GIFTS
FOR KIDS TO MAI

hamlyn

Cheryl Owen

GIFTS
FOR KIDS TO MAKE

An Hachette UK Company
www.hachette.co.uk

First published in Great Britain in 2006 by Hamlyn,
a division of Octopus Publishing Group Ltd.,
Endeavour House, 189 Shaftesbury Avenue,
London, WC2H 8JY
www.octopusbooksusa.com

This edition published in 2013

Distributed in the US by Hachette Book Group USA,
237 Park Avenue, New York NY 10017 USA

Distributed in Canada by Canadian Manda Group,
165 Dufferin Street, Toronto, Ontario, Canada
M6K 3H6

Cheryl Owen asserts the moral right to be identified
as the author of this work.

ISBN: 978-0-600-62515-5

Printed and bound in China

10 9 8 7 6 5 4 3 2 1

contents

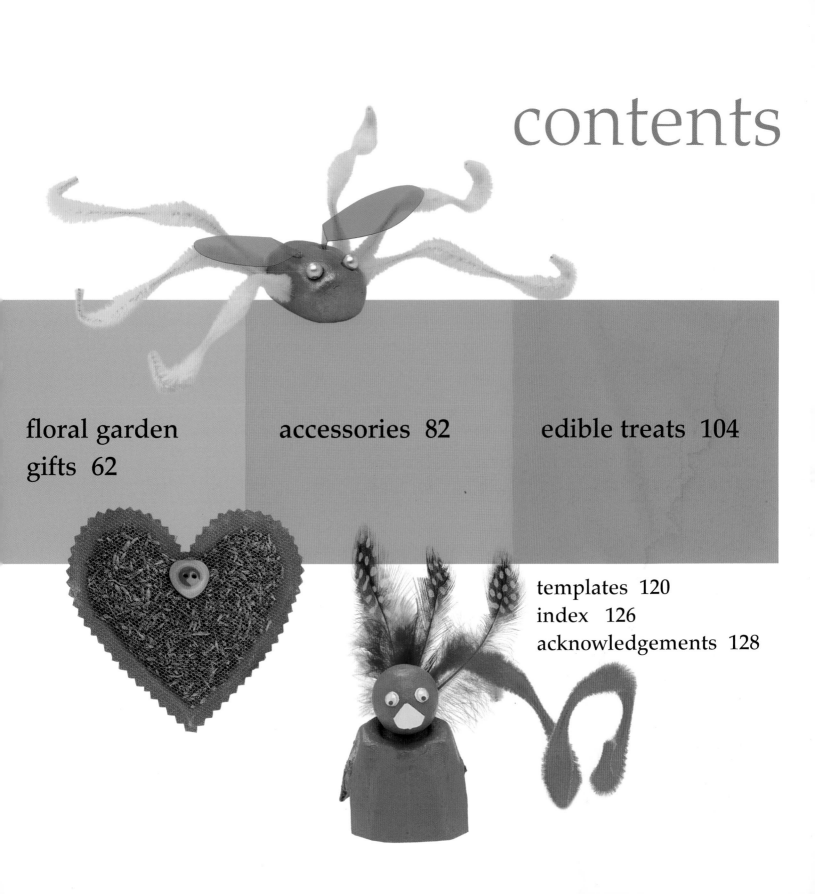

introduction

Children love being creative, and this book contains masses of super gifts for youngsters aged from three to ten years old to make for family and friends. There are ideas to mark every special occasion, from birthdays to Christmas, and projects that incorporate favourite traditional crafts as well as plenty of new ones, too. Once children have gained in confidence by making some of the projects, they can have fun adapting the ideas to create their own wonderful designs.

creative ideas for kids

This book encourages youngsters to learn lots of new skills. Apart from the many creative craft possibilities contained within the covers, it helps children appreciate how very rewarding it is to give to others; the joy of giving seems particularly special when the gift is something kids have made themselves. The crafts covered cater to all interests. There are projects to appeal to children who enjoy getting messy, involving clay and salt-dough modelling, and others that suit those of a neat and tidy nature, including sewing and working with pressed flowers. There are also simple cooking projects and more unusual hobbies, such as making candles and fragrant toiletries.

about this book

Here you will find six themed chapters of inspiring projects, each one accompanied by ideas for variations. Few special materials or tools are required, and all the projects have clear step-by-step instructions and photographs. Easy-to-use templates appear at the back of the book. Adult supervision is always advisable, especially for projects that incorporate cooking or using sharp tools. Guides to the age range and time needed are given with each project, but they are loose guides, so be led by your child's abilities.

safety tips

★ When buying tools or materials, always check they are safe for children and non-toxic.

★ Keep the room well ventilated when working with adhesive, acrylic paint and cosmetic colours. Wash hands well with soap and water after use.

★ Supervise young or less careful children carefully if a project calls for knives, sharp scissors, a needle or cooking over heat.

★ Never leave scissors open or lying where younger children or pets can reach them.

★ Always stick needles and pins into a pin cushion or a scrap of cloth when not in use.

★ Cover work surfaces with newspaper or an old cloth, preferably plastic. Plastic bags cut open and laid flat make a good water-resistant surface. Keep kitchen towels or rags at hand to mop up spills. Protect clothing with an apron or wear old clothes.

★ Wash paintbrushes immediately after use: modern paints dry quickly and dried-on paint can ruin a brush. Replace tops on pens, paint and glue containers.

materials

At the start of each project is a list of all the items you need, many of which you will already have around the house. Remember that all sorts of materials can be recycled for craftwork, such as glass jars, egg cartons, kitchen roll and snack tubes. Also, keep odd buttons and scraps of fabric, ribbons, lace, beads and sequins.

paper and card

Many projects use small amounts of paper or card. Save coloured tissue, gift wrap and unusual packaging to recycle into stationery. Interesting effects can be achieved by punching holes and cutting with deckle-edged and zig-zag scissors. Crepe paper is cheaply available at stationers and craft shops. Corrugated card from packaging can be painted in bright colours.

paint and pens

Acrylic paint is recommended for most of the painted projects. Although it is not the cheapest paint, a little goes a long way, the colours mix easily and dry quickly, and it is non-toxic. Poster paint is inexpensive, readily available and suits many paper, card and clay projects. Source paint for decorating ceramics and fabric at art shops, cosmetic colours from craft shops or soap-making websites. Many ceramic paints can be fixed by heating in an oven (this makes the object dishwasher-proof) – follow the manufacturer's instructions. Felt-tipped pens are quick and fun to use.

glue

Paper glue in stick form suits tissue, paper and card. Very strong, non-toxic PVA glue is used in many projects, including to make papier-mâché. All-purpose household glue (choose the non-toxic form) is quite strong and can stick many materials.

modelling materials

Air-drying clay can be rolled, modelled or shaped over a mould such as a bowl. Leave to harden, then paint. Polymer clay comes in many colours; why not mix them for a marbled effect? This clay is hardened by baking. Salt dough is made from plain flour, salt and water. Younger children enjoy stamping out shapes with cookie cutters. Once modelled, bake very slowly in the oven. Paint when cool. Applying a few coats of varnish prolongs the life of a baked salt-dough item, but don't display in a steamy or damp place!

craft items

Coloured pipecleaners are fun for children to bend and coil. Flexible plastic drinking straws are also surprisingly versatile. Cut them into slices to use as beads or bend over the ends to make stems for paper flowers. Nature provides many interesting craft materials including garden flowers and leaves for pressing and pebbles for creating characters. Save pumpkin and melon seeds to make jewellery, shells to form mobiles. Try craft shops for cheap cotton pulp balls to paint or colour, comical joggle eyes, and stickers that allow children of any age to achieve a professional finish. Thin neoprene foam comes in lovely colours and is easy to cut and decorate with felt-tipped pens. Clockworks are simple to fix to make smart clocks. Buy specialist soap- and candle-making materials here too.

glitter

Many adults can't resist twinkling glittery materials, but kids especially adore them. Leave glitter paint (adhesive with glitter suspended in it) to dry completely before handling. Traditional glitter is fun too: apply PVA glue where desired then sprinkle over glitter. Shake off the excess and leave to dry. Use a small paintbrush or cocktail stick to apply glue when only a tiny amount of glitter is required.

bric-a-brac

fridge magnets

ages 8–10 years

This jaunty pirate would make a super present for Father's Day. The character is made from polymer clay, which is baked until hard in the oven.

1 Roll a 3 cm (1¼ in) wide ball of salmon pink clay for the face. Flatten the ball. Roll a small ball of the same coloured clay for the nose. Press the nose to the centre of the face.

2 Roll two small balls of black clay for the moustache. Pull one side of each ball upward. Press each one to the face beneath the nose.

3 Using a rolling pin, roll more black clay out to a 3 mm (⅛ in) thickness on a pastry board. Use the templates on page 123 to cut out an eye patch and tricorn hat from the clay. Position the eye patch on the face to one side of the nose.

4 Roll a thin sausage of black clay for the eye-patch strap and place across the face, just above the patch. Position the tricorn hat at an angle over the top of the face.

**time needed
1 hour**
(excluding baking and cooling time)

what you need

Salmon pink and black polymer clay

Rolling pin

Pastry board

Small metal ring (from old or broken piece of jewellery)

PVA glue

Fridge magnet

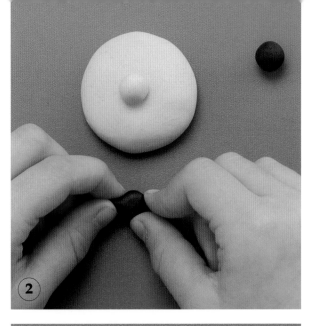

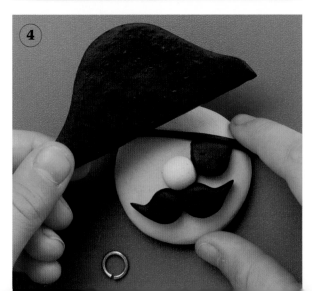

(5) Slip the small metal ring to peep out from one side of the hat as an earring, then press the hat down.

6 Bake the pirate in the oven following the clay manufacturer's instructions (an adult should help). When ready, remove from the oven and leave to cool, then glue a fridge magnet to the back.

tip
★ Wash your hands before using a new colour so you don't stain the clay.

variations

teddy

Make teddy's head by flattening a 3 cm (1¼ in) ball of caramel-coloured clay, then press on three smaller balls for his ears and snout. Roll three even smaller balls of black clay for the eyes and nose. Make a bow tie from two triangles of green clay decorated with smaller balls of pink clay. Mark the ears with the handle end of a paintbrush and draw a mouth with a knife.

strawberry

Mould a strawberry shape from a 3 cm (1¼ in) ball of red clay. To make the leaves, flatten a 2.5 cm (1 in) ball of green clay, cut in half and pare away V shapes in the curved edge. Press the leaves and stalk to the top of the strawberry. Mark seed shapes with the handle end of a paintbrush.

flowers

Press six balls of red or purple clay around a central ball of similar-sized yellow clay. Flatten the 'petals' slightly and dent them with the handle end of a paintbrush. Press six small balls of green clay around the centre of the flower.

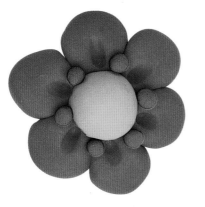

butterfly coaster

ages 4–5 years

Turn an ordinary opaque wall tile into a smart coaster for the table by sponging ceramic paint around a butterfly stencil. Marvel at how the butterfly emerges when you peel away the sticky-paper template. If you have time, you might like to make a set of coasters, each one a slightly different shade of green.

1 Trace the butterfly template on page 123, then transfer the design onto thin card. Cut out the shape and draw around it on the sticky-backed plastic using a felt-tipped pen. (An adult may need to help with the cutting.)

2 Carefully peel off the backing paper – again, an adult might be needed to prevent it from becoming tangled – then stick the butterfly to the centre of the ceramic tile.

3 Dampen the natural sponge with a little water. Brush the green ceramic paint onto the sponge using a large paintbrush; don't put the paint on too heavily.

4 Dab the paint all over the tile, then set it aside to dry.

5 Peel off the stencil to reveal the butterfly shape beneath.

what you need

Pencil

Tracing paper

Thin card

Scissors

Felt-tipped pen

Sticky-backed plastic

10 cm (4 in) opaque ceramic tile

Natural sponge

Large paintbrush

Green ceramic paint

⑤

variations

oak leaf

Using the template on page 123, cut an oak leaf from sticky-backed plastic. Stick the leaf to a yellow tile, then sponge on red and white ceramic paint. Once the paint is dry, peel off the stencil.

stripes

Stick lengths of masking tape across a large tile in long stripes. Paint the gaps between the pieces of tape with ceramic paint. Leave to dry, then peel off the tape.

tips

★ If you prefer a deeper colour, after allowing the first coat of paint to dry sponge on another layer of paint.

★ Make sure the sponge is not too wet before coating it with paint.

★ Wash the brush after use to prevent the bristles from hardening.

cherry bowl

ages 8–10 years

This pretty bowl is decorated with clay cherries that look good enough to eat. The contrasting laced effect is made by threading fine red braid or ribbon through holes made with a drinking straw before the vessel dries.

1 Turn the small bowl upside down on the pastry board and smear the outside with the petroleum jelly (this makes it easier to slide the clay off later).

2 Using the rolling pin, roll the air-drying clay flat on the pastry board until it is about 5 mm (¼ in) thick. Lay the clay over the bowl, smoothing it over the sides. Cut the clay level around the edge with the knife.

3 Make holes around the edge of the clay using the drinking straw.

4 Roll two 2 cm (¾ in) balls of clay between your palms into cherry shapes. Make a dent across the top of each one with the paintbrush. Flatten the cherries slightly.

5 Cut a wooden cocktail stick in half with the scissors. Push each half into the top of a cherry as a stalk. Set the bowl and cherries aside to harden overnight.

6 Slide the bowl off the mould. Wipe off any remaining jelly with kitchen towel. Glue the cherries inside the bowl close to the inside edge. Leave to set.

7 Paint the bowl deep yellow and the cherries red with green stalks. Leave to dry.

8 Lace the braid through the holes around the edge of the bowl and tie the ends together.

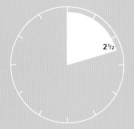

**time needed
2½ hours**
(excluding drying time)

what you need

Small bowl (to use as a mould)

Pastry board

Petroleum jelly (Vaseline)

Rolling pin

Air-drying clay

Knife

Drinking straw

Medium paintbrush

Wooden cocktail stick

Scissors

Kitchen towel

All-purpose household glue

Deep yellow, red and green acrylic paint

Fine red braid

(1)

variation

citrus bowl

At the end of step 2 cut a wavy edge around the clay bowl. Roll five 2.5 cm (1 in) balls of clay to make oranges and lemons. Squeeze the edges of two balls to form lemons. Flatten the remaining balls slightly to make oranges. When the clay has hardened, glue the fruit around the inner edge of the bowl, leave to set, then paint the bowl green and the fruit orange and yellow.

(2)

(6)

tips

★ Rest the cherries on pencil erasers or something similar inside the bowl while the glue dries.

★ Place a circle of greaseproof paper or a doily in the bowl if it's to be used for sweets that don't have wrappers.

bird clock

ages 8–10 years

If you colour in the lid of a box using bright paints, you can transform it into a fabulous clock. Paint a simple bird on the face, add the flourish of a real feather tail and you have your very own version of a cuckoo clock.

1 Paint the cardboard box lid with the yellow paint and leave it to dry. Trace the clock template on page 120 onto tracing paper. Lightly tape the tracing paper to the box using masking tape.

2 One by one, slip the four round stickers beneath the tracing paper and stick them at each quarter-hour position. Carefully remove the tracing paper.

3 Using the template on page 120, draw a bird beneath the clock in pencil, then paint it in purple and pink shades.

4 When the paint has dried, glue a feather to the back of the bird to make a tail.

5 Make a hole through the centre of the clock with the sharp point of the scissors (an adult might need to help). Make the hole large enough to accommodate the clockwork mechanism. Fix the clockwork through the hole (follow the manufacturer's instructions), then fit the hands to the clock.

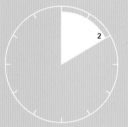

**time needed
2 hours**
(excluding drying time)

what you need

Cardboard box lid about 23 x 17 cm (9 x 6¾ in)

Large and medium paintbrushes

Sunshine yellow, purple and pink acrylic paint

Pencil

Tracing paper

Masking tape

4 round stickers

PVA glue

Feather

Sharp-edged scissors

Clockwork mechanism and hands

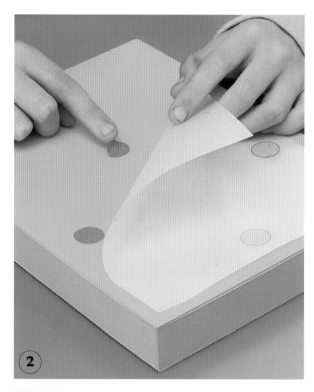

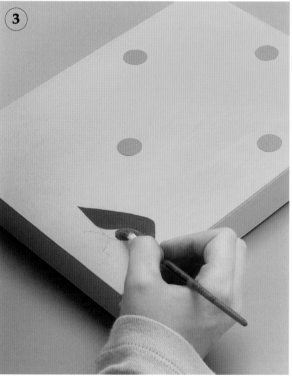

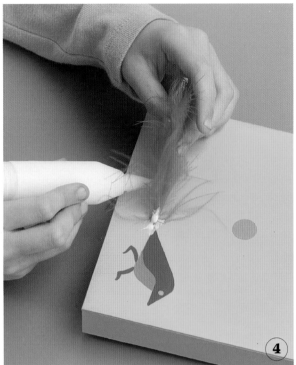

tips

★ Masking tape is very useful if you want to tape something temporarily in place because the tape can easily be removed when you've finished with it.

★ Paint the clock hands if you would prefer them to be a different colour.

variation

bullseye clock

Paint different-coloured rings on a round cardboard box lid to resemble a target. Use the clock template as before, but this time stick silver star stickers at the quarter positions before removing the tracing paper. Finally, fit the clockwork mechanism and hands.

ladybird paper-weight

ages 3–5 years

This giant ladybird is not only great to look at but very useful, too, for keeping papers and letters weighted in place. The ladybird is very easy to make from air-drying clay, which hardens overnight ready for you to paint brightly next day.

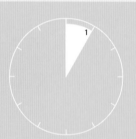

time needed
1 hour
(excluding drying time)

what you need

Air-drying clay

Red, black and blue acrylic paint

Medium paintbrush

(1) Roll a ball of clay about 4.5 cm (1¾ in) wide between your palms. Roll the ball into an oval, then flatten it slightly. Set this ladybird shape aside to dry, which takes about a day.

(2) Paint the ladybird red with a paintbrush and leave the paint to dry.

(3) Paint the front of the ladybird black for its head. Paint a line along the centre of the back to divide the wings. Paint a black circle on each wing.

4 When the black paint has dried, make dots for eyes on the ladybird's head with blue paint. Leave the ladybird to dry.

1

2

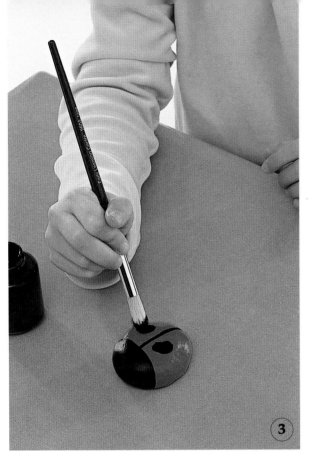

variations

bumble bee

Make the body of the bumble bee in the same way as the ladybird. Then roll two ovals of clay for the wings. Squeeze one side of the wings to a point. Wet the wings and the top of the bumble bee with a little water, then press the wings in place. Leave overnight to dry, then paint the body yellow. Leave to dry, then finish by painting black stripes and white wings.

tips

★ Keep air-drying clay in an air-tight container to stop it from drying out.

★ Glue on sequins or beads for eyes, if you wish.

★ Always wet both pieces of clay with water when you join pieces together (and do it before the clay has hardened).

tortoise

Start by making the body of the tortoise in the same way as the ladybird. Score lines on the shell with a clay modelling tool, as shown in the picture. To make the head, tail and legs, roll logs of clay then join them to the underside of the body as for the bee wings (see above). Squeeze the tail tip to a point and rest the head on a pencil while the clay dries.

hen egg cosy

ages 8–10 years

Here is a charming hen that would make a lovely Easter present. She's very useful too, helping to keep a breakfast boiled egg nice and warm. The hen is made from coloured felt, which is easy to sew because the edges do not fray.

1 Trace the hen, beak and comb templates on page 122 then transfer the designs onto thin card. Cut out the shapes and draw around them with a felt-tipped pen as follows: a pair of hens on the fawn felt, a beak on the yellow felt and a comb on the red felt. Cut out the shapes.

(2) Thread the needle with the blue thread, tying a knot in the end, then sew one blue bead on each of the hens, on the outer side where the cross is marked on the template. These will be the eyes.

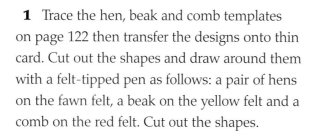

(3) Fold the beak in half along the broken line on the template. Pin the folded edge onto the wrong side of one hen (the side without the bead), between the dots on the side of the template.

(4) Pin the comb above the beak, at the top of the hen's head, between the dots on the top of the template.

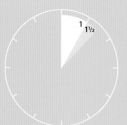

**time needed
1–1½ hours**

what you need

Pencil

Tracing paper

Thin card

Scissors

Felt-tipped pen

23 cm (9 in) square of fawn-coloured felt

10 cm (4 in) squares of yellow- and red-coloured felt

Sewing needle

Blue sewing thread

Two blue beads

Dressmaking pins

Red stranded cotton embroidery thread

6

5 Pin the hens together with the wrong sides facing each other (on the inside). Make sure the beads are on the outside and in line with each other.

6 Thread the needle with six strands of red embroidery thread (an adult might need to help to prevent tangles) and tie a knot in the end. Sew the hens together using running stitch (push the needle up from the back of the fabric to the front; pull the thread through, then push the needle from front to back a little way forward to make a straight line). Make sure you keep a 5 mm (¼ in) border between your stitches and the outside edge. (An adult might need to help.) Remove the pins.

tip
★ Make sure you sew the eyes on the opposite sides of each hen to make a matching pair of hen pieces.

variations

yellow chick
Make this cuddly chick from yellow fleece in the same way as you made the hen but leaving off the comb. Give the chick an orange beak and black bead eyes and sew it together with orange embroidery thread.

blue hen
Choose unusual colour combinations such as this blue hen with a bright pink comb and pink eyes.

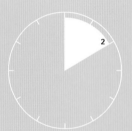

**time needed
2 hours**
(excluding drying time)

what you need

Cardboard snack tube

Kitchen paper tube

Sweetie tube

Large and medium
paintbrushes

Acrylic paint in shades
of dark blue, light
blue, turquoise,
orange, peach
and pink

Pair of compasses
and pen

Thick card

Scissors

All-purpose household
glue

desk tidy

ages 5–6 years

Brighten an untidy desk with this smart desk tidy. Save snack, kitchen paper and sweetie tubes to make the tidy, paint them in brilliant colours, then fill with pencils, pens and rulers. This makes a perfect present for a busy office worker or budding artist.

1 Remove the lids from the cardboard tubes and paint the inside of each tube at the top in one of the colours, then paint the outside the same colour. Leave them to dry.

2 Paint wavy bands around the outside of the tubes in contrasting colours.

3 Using the pair of compasses and pen, draw a 14 cm (5¾ in) diameter circle on the piece of card. (An adult might need to help.)

4 Draw a wavy edge inside the circle to create the base. Cut out the base and paint it. Leave it to dry.

5 Run a line of glue inside the bottom of the kitchen paper tube and stand it on the base. Glue first the snack tube, then the sweetie tube to the base and to the kitchen paper tube. Let the glue harden and dry before using.

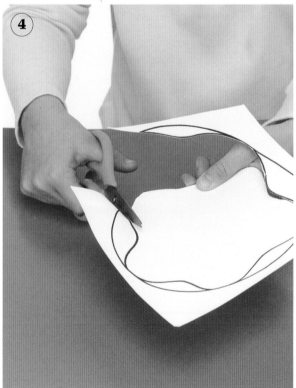

variation

money tube

Remove the lid of a cardboard snack tube. Cut a slot in the base; this is now the top of the money tube. Paint the tube light blue all over and leave to dry. Paint bright blue waves around the bottom of the tube and use a sponge to dab white paint above the waves as clouds. Paint a few seagulls in between. Replace the lid on the bottom of the tube.

(5)

tips

★ Don't forget to cover the surface that you're working on with old newspaper or with a plastic tablecloth.

★ Decorated cardboard snack tubes can also make effective pencil cases and unusual treasure boxes.

snowman decoration

ages 4–6 years

Salt dough is fun to make as well as to model with. This happy salt-dough snowman makes a lovely Christmas present or tree decoration. Left-over dough can be kept in the refrigerator for about five days.

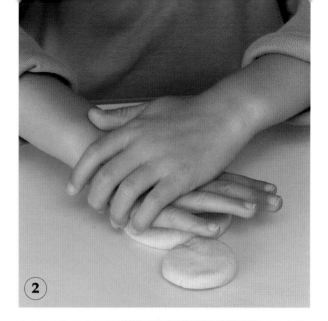

1 Mix the flour and the salt in the bowl. Gradually add the water until you have a firm, pliable dough. Set aside for ten minutes.

2 Place the dough on the pastry board and roll a 4 cm (1½ in) wide ball for the body and a 3 cm (1¼ in) wide ball for the head. Flatten the body and head.

3 Lay the body and head on baking parchment, butting them together. With the rolling pin roll a scrap of dough to a 5 mm (¼ in) thickness. Cut a rectangle about 4 x 3 cm (1½ x 1¼ in) for the hat. Press to the head.

4 Roll four logs 1 cm (½ in) thick. Lay one across the hat as a brim. Lay another across the 'neck' as a scarf. Lay the other logs at angles to the scarf, touching at the top, and dent the ends for a fringe with the knife.

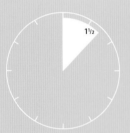

1½

**time needed
1½ hours**
(plus 6 hours for cooking)

what you need

6 tablespoons plain flour

3 tablespoons salt

Mixing bowl

3 tablespoons water

Pastry board

Baking parchment

Rolling pin

Blunt knife

Drinking straw

Baking sheet

Acrylic paint in shades
of white, orange,
green, red and purple

Medium and fine
paintbrushes

Narrow ribbon

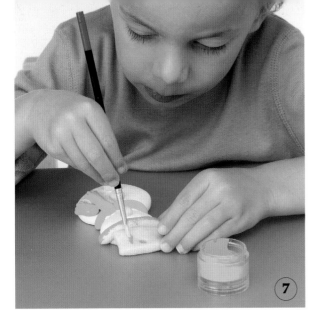

(7)

5 Roll three small balls of dough, press one to the head as a nose, the others to the body as buttons. Make a hole at the top of the hat with the straw.

6 Place the snowman on baking parchment on a baking sheet. Place in a preheated oven, 120°C (250°F), Gas Mark ½, for about six hours, until hard. Leave to cool in the oven.

(7) Paint the snowman's body white. Paint the hat, scarf, nose and buttons. Add a smile and two eyes. Leave to dry then thread the ribbon through the hole and tie.

tip
★ Give salt-dough models a few coats of varnish for protection.

variations

reindeer

Roll the dough to a 5 mm (¼ in) thickness. Stamp a reindeer with a cookie cutter. Punch a hole with a straw for hanging. Bake for about four hours, leave to cool and paint. Tie two bells around the reindeer's neck with silver elastic. Hang from a piece of ribbon.

tree

Roll the dough to a 5 mm (¼ in) thickness. Stamp a tree with a cookie cutter. Punch a hole with a straw for hanging. Press small balls of dough to the tree as baubles. Bake for about four hours, leave to cool and paint. Apply glitter to the baubles. Hang from a piece of ribbon.

striped cat napkin ring

ages 5–6 years

Amuse guests with a set of cute striped cat napkin rings at a celebration meal. They can take their cats home with them to remind them of the wonderful time they've had. If you make one for each guest, you could even write names on the cat's tummy so everyone knows where to sit.

1 Cut out one section from the egg box. Glue a cotton pulp ball on top for the head.

2 Trace the cat ear template on page 123 then transfer the design twice onto thin card. Cut out the ears, fold them in half and glue them to the top of the head.

3 Paint the cat pale orange. Leave to dry.

4 Glue the red pompom to the head as a nose. Draw eyes with the black felt-tipped pen.

5 Draw furry patterns over the cat with the orange felt-tipped pen. Make a hole at the back of the body and glue the orange pipecleaner inside it for the tail. When you lay the table, wind the tail around a napkin.

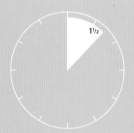

**time needed
1½ hours**

what you need

Cardboard egg box

All-purpose household glue

3 cm (1½ in) cotton pulp ball

Pencil

Tracing paper

Thin card

Scissors

Medium paintbrush

Pale orange acrylic paint

5 mm (¼ in) red pompom

Black and orange felt-tipped pens

Orange pipecleaner

26

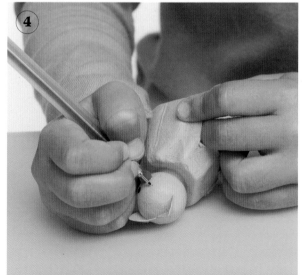

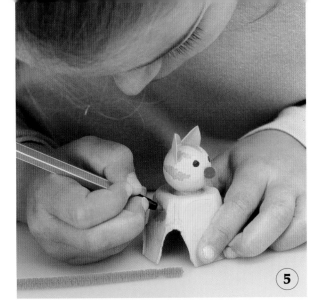

(5)

variations

bird

In step 2, use the template on page 123 to cut a beak, fold it in half and glue to the front of the head. Paint the beak yellow and the bird blue. Leave to dry, then stick on two joggle eyes. Glue feathers and chenille pipecleaners to the back of the bird, winding one pipecleaner around a napkin.

elephant

In step 2, use the template on page 123 to cut two ears from pink card, then glue to the sides of the head. Paint the elephant pale pink. Make a hole in the front of the head. Glue a pale pink pipecleaner into the hole for a trunk. Draw eyes with a black pen. Wind the trunk around a napkin.

snowman

Paint the body and head white. Cut a strip of felt, using zig-zag scissors along one long edge. Glue around the head. Stick a pompom to the head as a nose. Draw eyes with black pen. Glue a button to the front of the snowman. Wrap a pipecleaner around the neck as a scarf, winding the end around a napkin.

tip
★ Cotton pulp balls are cheap to buy from craft shops.

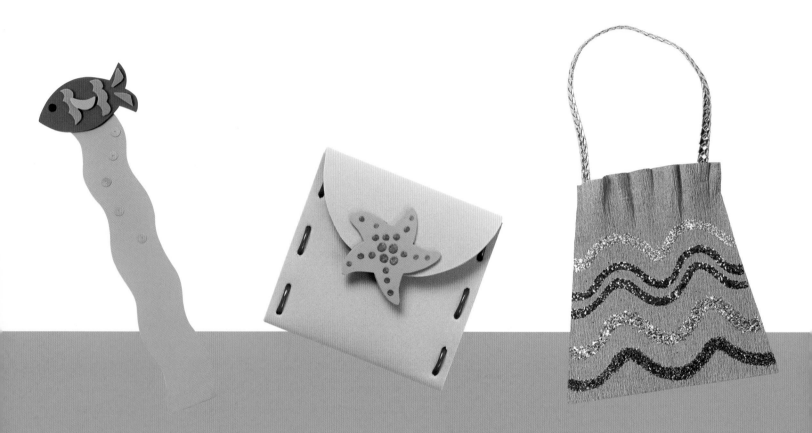

stationery

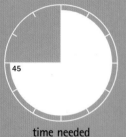

what you need

Pencil

Tracing paper

Thin card

Scissors

Black felt-tipped pen

Aquamarine, blue and bright pink neoprene foam

All-purpose household glue

5 silver sequins

fishy bookmark

ages 5–6 years

A wavy bookmark decorated with a foam fish is a great gift for a keen reader, and looks sweet as it pokes out from the top of the pages. Add more sparkle by sticking on silver sequins to look like bubbles. If you have lots of foam and fancy a more adventurous project, try making the pretty purse shown in the variations opposite.

1 Trace the bookmark template on page 125 then transfer the design onto thin card. Cut out the shape and draw around it on the aquamarine foam with the black felt-tipped pen. Similarly, cut a fish from the blue foam. Draw an eye on the fish with the black felt-tipped pen.

2 Using the template on page 125, cut scales and tail details from the bright pink foam and a fin from aquamarine foam.

3 Glue the scales and tail details, then the fin, onto the fish. Glue the fish to the top of the bookmark.

4 As a finishing touch, glue silver sequins to the bookmark as bubbles. Leave the bookmark to dry before using.

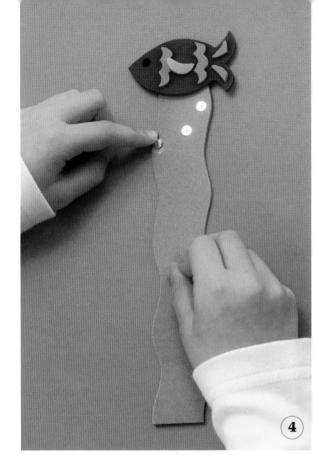

(4)

tips

★ It's easy to colour the foam using felt-tipped pens.

★ If you're not happy with your first try at cutting out the fish or shell template, have another go until you get it right.

variations

shell bookmark

Cut a 20 x 3.5 cm (8 x 1⅜ in) strip of yellow foam. Use the template on page 125 to cut a shell from red foam. Glue the shell to the yellow strip. Paint green lines on the shell and spots on the bookmark.

pink purse

Cut out a purse shape from pink foam using the template on page 125. Fold the front up along the broken lines on the template and sew at the sides with plastic thonging (an adult might need to help to keep it neat). Fasten the flap at the front by sticking on a hook and loop fastening spot (available from craft shops). As a finishing touch, cut a starfish from aquamarine foam using the template on page 125, glue onto the flap and dot with bright pink paint.

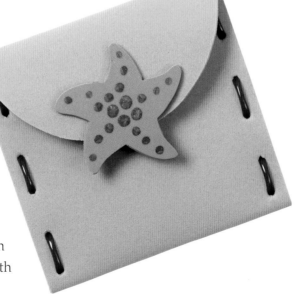

paper handbag

ages 5–6 years

Slip a secret message or a tiny light-weight present into a pretty handbag decorated with colourful sequins. Use these paper creations as party bags for small, thin gifts, such as stickers and hair accessories. Friends are sure to love them! As a plus, the bag can be hung up and so makes a super Christmas tree decoration.

1 Cut a 20 x 10 cm (8 x 4 in) rectangle of crepe paper, cutting the long edge parallel with the ridges on the paper. Fold the paper in half.

(2) Using a pencil and ruler, draw slanted edges from the fold out to the top corners. Cut along the slanted edges.

(3) Gently stretch both sides of the top to make a pretty frilled edge.

(4) Glue the slanted edges together. Glue one end of the braid inside each corner of the top of the bag to make a handle.

(5) Decorate by sticking rows of sequins across the front of the bag.

**time needed
45 minutes**

what you need

Scissors

Pencil

Ruler

Crepe paper

All-purpose household glue

20 cm (8 in) narrow red braid

Shaped sequins

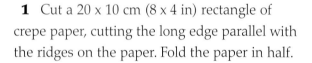

variations

lilac handbag

Fold the paper rectangle in step 1 but do not cut slanted side edges or stretch the top of the bag. Glue the sides together, then give the bag a beaded braid handle. Glue lilac marabou trim around the top edge and decorate by sticking a few silver sequins on the front.

turquoise handbag

In step 2 draw slanted side edges down and outward from the top edge to the fold. Gently stretch both sides of the top to make a frilled edge. Glue the sides together, then give the bag a gold braid handle. Apply wavy lines of glitter across the bag.

tips

★ Crepe paper folds more neatly if you draw along the fold line first with a pencil.

★ Try using double-layered crepe paper: it's stronger than a single layer and allows you to have a different colour showing on each side.

button bear card

ages 3–5 years

Buttons come in so many colours, shapes and sizes and you are sure to have some spare ones at home. Have fun arranging the most colourful and unusual in different shapes to make amusing characters like this cute bear on a greetings card.

1 Cut a 20 x 10 cm (8 x 4 in) rectangle of cream card to make the greetings card and fold it in half. Glue a pink button with four holes to the front of the card to make the bear's head.

2 Glue a larger red button beneath the head to make the body.

3 Stick two mauve buttons on each side of the body to form legs.

4 Glue two smaller purple buttons on each side at the top of the head to make ears. Finally, glue a very small pale pink button to the bottom of the head to create the bear's muzzle. Allow the glue to dry before writing inside the card.

45

time needed
45 minutes

what you need

Ruler

Pencil

Scissors

Cream card

Selection of flat buttons

All-purpose household glue

(2)

(3)

variations

dolphin card

Glue a dolphin-shaped button to the front of a pale blue card folded in half as before. Stick torn strips of bright blue and yellow paper across the card to create the sea and sand. To complete the picture, sew two shell-shaped buttons to the sand, being careful not to crease the card (an adult might need to help).

piggy card

Tear strips of lilac and spotty green paper, then glue them across the front of a pale blue folded card to make the sky and a field. Carefully sew three piggy-shaped buttons to the field.

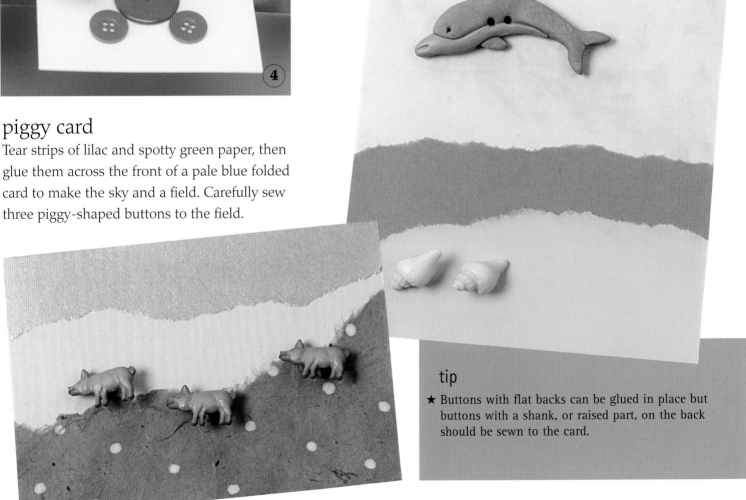

tip

★ Buttons with flat backs can be glued in place but buttons with a shank, or raised part, on the back should be sewn to the card.

decorated notebook

ages 6–8 years

Ordinary notebooks are cheap to buy, but you can make them look very expensive by decorating them with strips of coloured paper. Save wrapping paper from birthdays and old scraps of wallpaper and tear out pages from glossy magazines with striking images. Cut the edges of some of the papers with deckle and zig-zag scissors for extra interest.

1 Using the pen and ruler, draw lines on the plain and patterned papers, marking them into strips. Cut out the strips with the deckle-edged, zig-zag or ordinary scissors.

2 Glue the strips to the front of the notebook and along the spine, leaving the ends extending above and below the cover.

3 Open the book and glue the ends of the strips to the inside of the cover and spine.

4 Measure the inside of the covers and, using ordinary scissors, cut two pieces of patterned paper to fit inside the covers. Glue the papers inside the covers to hide the ends of the strips. Leave open to dry.

45

time needed
45 minutes

what you need

Pen

Ruler

Plain and patterned papers

Scissors: deckle-edged, zig-zag and ordinary

Paper glue

Thick notebook with a spine

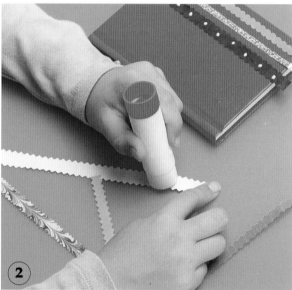

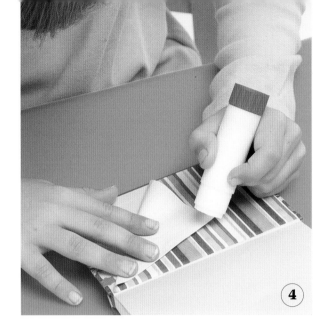

(4)

variations

striped writing paper and paper squares notelet

Glue gift-wrapping ribbon and strips of patterned papers along one edge of a piece of writing paper. Glue squares of patterned papers to the front of a notelet. Leave to dry before using.

spotty writing paper and envelope

Attach round stickers to the top of a piece of writing paper. Reserve another sticker to fasten the envelope.

ribbon, sequin and ric-rac notelet

Glue lengths of patterned ribbon and ric-rac and a string of sequins in stripes to the front of a notelet. Set aside until completely dry.

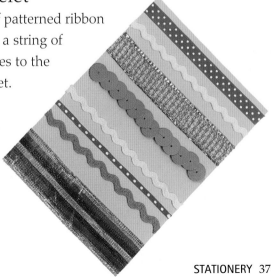

tip

★ Fold sheets of writing paper in half to make notelets, then decorate them.

star gift wrap

ages 4–6 years

Create beautiful gift wrap by stamping a stunning star onto coloured paper using a potato. Make a matching gift tag by cutting around a star, punching a hole in it, and threading with contrasting ribbon or sparkling braid.

45

**time needed
45 minutes**

what you need

Large potato

Pencil

Tracing paper

Thin card

Scissors

Black felt-tipped pen

Knife

Green, blue and pink acrylic paint

Paintbrush

Large sheets of yellow paper

Pale green paper

Scissors

Hole punch

Narrow ribbon

38

(1) Cut the potato in half lengthways to give a wide, flat surface. Trace the star template on page 121 then transfer the design onto thin card. Cut out the star and draw around it on one of the cut surfaces using a black felt-tipped pen. Score the star shape with a knife, then pare away the potato around it to leave a raised star. (An adult might need to help.)

2 Carefully dab green paint on the star with the paintbrush.

3 Stamp the star onto the sheet of yellow paper. Repeat, stamping stars in the same colour all over the paper, adding more paint to the stamp if necessary.

4 Wash the stamp and paintbrush. Brush blue paint onto the stamp and stamp stars in gaps on the paper. Then stamp a star onto a piece of pale green paper to make a gift tag.

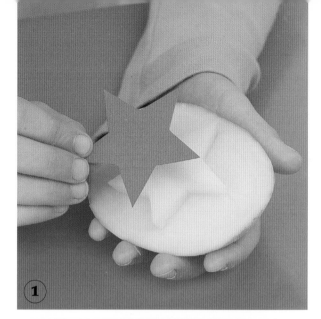
①

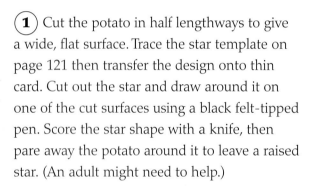
⑤

⑥

(7)

(5) Wash the stamp and paintbrush again. Brush the potato with the pink paint.

(6) Stamp pink stars in gaps on the yellow paper. Leave to dry.

(7) To make the tag, cut out the star on the green paper, leaving a gap around the edge. Punch a hole in the tag and thread with the ribbon, knotting the ends.

variations

moon and star gift tag

Using the templates on page 121, cut cloud and moon shapes into the two flat surfaces of a cut potato. Apply silver paint to the cloud and print onto a pale blue gift tag. Leave to dry, then apply pink paint to the moon shape and print a moon on the tag. Stick on two silver star stickers. Apply pink glitter to the moon and dots of silver glitter around the moon and stars.

tip

★ Don't put too much paint on the potato stamp or you will lose the neat points of the star.

smiling sun gift tag

Using the template on page 121, cut a sun into a cut potato. Paint the sun with yellow paint and the rays with orange paint. Print onto a pink gift tag. When dry, draw a smiling face on the sun. Print spots around the sun by applying paint to the eraser at the end of a pencil.

floral gift tag

ages 6–8 years

Receiving a present is always a treat, and to have a handmade gift tag attached is a super finishing touch. This gift tag with its pretty flower in a plant pot is so easy to make because the flower is just a square of scrunched-up tissue paper.

1 Cut a 12 x 8.5 cm (4¾ x 3⅜ in) rectangle of white card for the gift tag and fold it in half. Trace the plant pot template on page 121 then transfer the design on to the red corrugated card. Cut out the pot.

2 Glue the plant pot to the front of the tag.

3 Draw a plant stem and leaves from the top of the plant pot with the green felt-tipped pen.

4 Cut a 4 cm (1½ in) square of pink tissue paper. Scrunch up the square and glue to the top of the stem.

5 Punch a hole in the top left corner of the gift tag. Thread the red ribbon through the hole ready to tie to the present.

.

45

**time needed
45 minutes**

what you need

Ruler

Pencil

Scissors

White card

Tracing paper

Red corrugated card

Paper glue

Green felt-tipped pen

Pink tissue paper

Hole punch

20 cm (8 in) narrow red ribbon

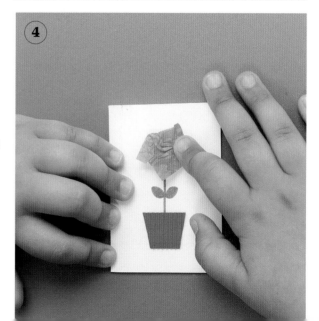

⑤

variations

tree in a tub picture

Cut a tub shape from pink corrugated card and glue it to a piece of cream card. Draw in the tree trunk with a green felt-tipped pen. Cut four 4 cm (1½ in) squares of green tissue paper and scrunch them to make the leaves. For the flowers cut out three 3 cm (1¼ in) squares of red tissue paper and scrunch them up. Glue the leaves then the flowers to the tree trunk. Glue the cream card to green chequered gift wrap and place inside a green picture frame.

tip

★ If you can't source coloured corrugated card, cut out a piece of plain card from an old box and paint it brightly.

yellow flower picture

Draw a row of three plant stems and leaves with a green felt-tipped pen on a piece of white card. Cut three 4 cm (1½ in) squares of yellow tissue paper, scrunch them up and glue to the stems. Stick the white card to red chequered gift wrap and place inside a picture frame.

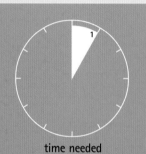

spotty dog card

ages 6–8 years

The head of this amusing character is attached with hook and loop spot fasteners so it can be removed and worn as a badge – the spot fasteners fix onto any woolly surface. (Buy them from craft shops.) As a variation you can make a pink pig or a funny frog.

1 Cut an 18 x 11 cm (7¼ x 4½ in) rectangle from the light brown card and fold it in half, parallel with the short edges. Trace the body template on page 122 then transfer the design to the folded card, matching the fold lines. Cut out the body. Cut a head and tail from light brown card too, using the templates provided.

2 Draw a mouth on the head with the black felt-tipped pen. Tear black paper into patches. Glue the patches to the head, body and tail.

3 Glue the black pompom to the middle of the head as a nose. Glue the joggle eyes above the nose.

4 Using the template on page 122, cut two ears from the black paper. Glue the ears behind the head. Fold the tips of the ears over the head.

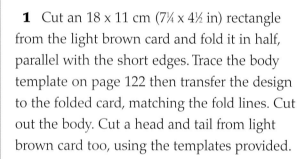

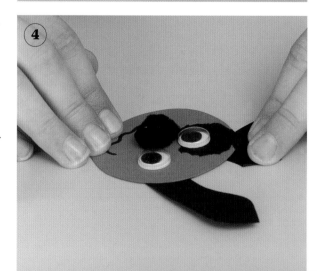

time needed
1 hour

what you need

Ruler

Pencil

Scissors

Light brown card

Tracing paper

Black felt-tipped pen

Black paper

PVA glue

Black pompom

2 joggle eyes

2 hook and loop
   spot fasteners

variations

pink pig card

Using the templates on pages 122–123, cut a body and pig head, muzzle and ears from pink card. Draw eyes on the head and nostrils on the muzzle with a black felt-tipped pen. Stick the ears to the back of the head, and bend forward. Stick the muzzle to the head using a foam adhesive pad. Make a hole on the back of the body and fix a pink curly pipecleaner inside it as a tail.

5

5 Glue the tail to the back of the body and fold it toward the front. Stick the soft spot fasteners to the top of the body. Stick the head on top with the rough spot fasteners.

tip

★ If you prefer, you can draw the dog's patches with a black felt-tipped pen instead of gluing on torn paper.

funny frog card

Use the templates on pages 122–123 to cut out the frog's body, head and two feet from green card. Draw a smile on the head with a black felt-tipped pen. Glue two joggle eyes to the head. Make two holes on the front of the body and through the feet and fix a green pipecleaner between them for legs.

scented gifts

fragrant sachet

ages 6–8 years

This fragrant drawer sachet keeps clothes smelling sweet. It is made from scraps of fabric and netting and you only need a handful of pot pourri or lavender to fill it. Cut out the heart shapes using zig-zag scissors to stop the edge of the fabrics from fraying. A heart-shaped button makes a delightful finishing touch.

1 Trace the heart template on page 124 then transfer the design onto thin card. Cut out the heart and draw around it with a black felt-tipped pen on the pink fabric and netting. Cut out both hearts with the zig-zag scissors.

(2) Use a cotton bud to run a line of glue around the outer edge of the pink fabric heart, leaving the top edge free from glue. Press the net heart on top. Hold in place while drying.

(3) Pour the pot pourri or lavender into the sachet through the hole in the top of the heart.

(4) Run another line of glue around the top of the fabric heart. Press the netting onto it firmly to close the sachet and prevent its contents from escaping. Finally, glue the heart-shaped button to the front of the sachet. Set aside to dry.

45

**time needed
45 minutes**

what you need

Pencil

Tracing paper

Thin card

Scissors

Black felt-tipped pen

Zig-zag scissors

Pink fabric

Pink netting

Cotton bud

PVA glue

Handful of pot pourri
 or dried lavender

Heart-shaped button

(2)

(3)

tips

★ Fill the sachet over a sheet of paper, then you can tip any spilt lavender or pot pourri mix back into its container.

★ Don't worry if you can't find a button that's heart-shaped; just go for one in a colour that matches.

★ Refresh pot pourri with 1–2 drops of essential oil of lavender every few months if the scent fades. (Have an adult on hand to prevent too many drops of essential oil from spilling out.)

4

variation

stars and flowers sachets

Cut out the fabric and netting in the shape of a star or flower, using the templates on page 124, then finish with a button matching the colour or shape of the sachet.

beeswax candle

ages 6–8 years

Roll an elegant candle from two coloured strips of beeswax, then enjoy the honey-sweet scent as it burns. Sheets of beeswax are available from craft shops or specialist candle-making suppliers and websites.

1

(1) Trace the candle template on page 124 twice, once along the narrow line and once along the wide line, then transfer the shapes onto thin card. Cut out the shapes and draw around the wide strip on the natural beeswax and the narrow strip on the red beeswax with a pencil. Cut out both strips. Lay the narrow red strip over the wide natural strip with the lower, long edges level.

(2) From the leftover natural beeswax, cut a piece about 2 x 2 cm (¾ x ¾ in). Roll it around one end of the wick.

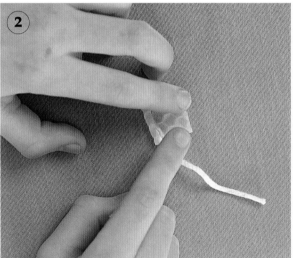

2

(3) Turn over the two beeswax strips and lay the wick along the longest side edge of the layered beeswax strips and start to roll the strips around the wick.

(4) Once you have finished rolling the candle, press the short ends of beeswax smoothly to the candle to prevent it from unravelling.

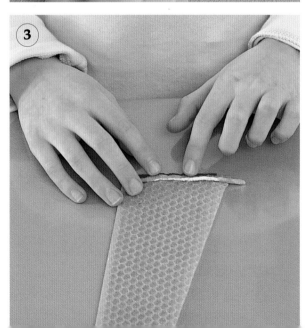

3

45

time needed
45 minutes

what you need

Pencil

Tracing paper

Thin card

Scissors

1 sheet natural beeswax

1 sheet red beeswax

9 cm (3¾ in) candle wick

(4)

variations

triple spiral candle

Roll three layers of beeswax in contrasting colours. Cut one wide strip of beeswax and one narrow strip as before, then cut a medium-width strip, each one in a different colour. Stack the strips with the bottom edges level, as before, then roll carefully around the wick.

straight beeswax candle

Coil two straight strips of red beeswax together around a wick. Cut the ends level and press them to the candle.

CAUTION Be very careful with lit candles. For safety, always ask an adult to light the candle and never leave a lit candle burning unattended.

appliqué candle

Appliqué wax, available from craft shops, is a thin layer of wax that can be cut out and stuck to candles. Cut a zig-zag strip of gold applique wax and a few triangles from gold and blue appliqué wax. Press the pieces in a pattern around a pink candle.

tip

★ Sheets of beeswax are best handled with warm hands and the beeswax is easier to roll if it is not cold. Warm the sheets with a hair drier if the room is cold.

bath salts

ages 6–7 years

It is very simple to make coloured bath salts for Mum or Granny by adding a tiny amount of cosmetic colouring to Epsom salts. Pour the salts into a clear container so the colour shows through and glue a flamboyant artificial flower to the lid as an attractive finishing touch. Even better, make your own flower decoration by following the instructions on pages 74–75.

1 Pour the Epsom salts into the final container to measure exactly the amount you need. Then tip them into a bowl.

2 Add one drop of vanilla essence to scent the salts. Stir the mixture with a tablespoon.

3 Add 2 drops each of the red and yellow cosmetic colourings. Be careful not to add more than this amount. Stir in the colouring until all the salts turn pale orange.

4 Spoon the mixture into the container. Screw the lid on tightly. Glue the artificial flower to the lid.

**time needed
45 minutes**

what you need

Approx. 200 g (7 oz)
  Epsom salts

Clear container with lid

Bowl

Vanilla essence

Tablespoon

Red and yellow
  cosmetic colourings

All-purpose household
  glue

Artificial flower

3

variation

two-tone bath salts

Colour the salts with a few drops of blue cosmetic colour to give a pale blue. Divide the salts in half, placing them in two bowls. Colour one half with a few more drops of blue cosmetic colour to give a deeper shade of blue. Holding the container at an angle, pour the dark blue salts into your container, then pour the pale blue salts on top, filling to the top. Screw on the lid. Glue an artificial flower on the lid, as before.

4

tips

★ Be extra careful not to colour your clothing and the floor!

★ Add less colour than you think you need – a few drops go a very long way. It's easy to add more colour if you need to, but impossible to take colour away.

★ Epsom salts are available from pharmacies and natural health stores.

★ Cosmetic colourings are available from craft stores and soap-making websites.

CAUTION Be careful not to get the Epsom salts on your skin, and wash your hands well with soap and water after finishing the project. Open a window to keep the room well ventilated while you work.

Epsom salts are not recommended for use by pregnant women, young children or people who have high blood pressure or heart disease.

lavender pillow

ages 8–10 years

Sweet-smelling lavender is known to help us sleep, so what better filling could there be for a pretty hand-painted pillow? Give it to a friend to keep on her bed, or to a tired parent who compains about lack of sleep.

1 Cut two 28 x 20 cm (11½ x 8 in) rectangles from the pink cotton fabric for the pillow-case. Trace the lavender sprigs template on page 120 and transfer it into the middle of one rectangle.

2 Paint over the stems of the lavender sprigs with the light green fabric paint, tracing over the pencil lines.

(3) Paint the flowers with the pale pink paint using the fine paintbrush. Leave the paint to dry, then iron the wrong side of the fabric to fix the paint, following the manufacturer's instructions.

(4) Cut the scallop-shaped lace in half. Pin each piece to the painted rectangle 5 cm (2 in) in from the two short edges. Thread up the needle with the cream-coloured thread, knot the end, and sew the lace in place using running stitch (see page 21). (An adult might need to help.) Remove the pins.

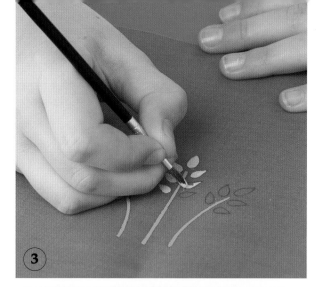

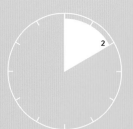

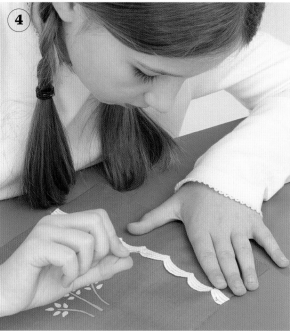

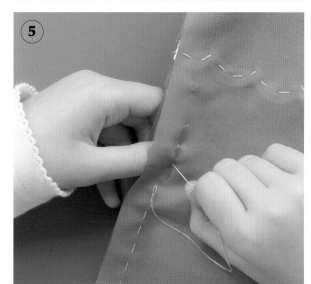

**time needed
2 hours**

what you need

Ruler

Pencil

Scissors

20 cm (8 in) of 90 cm (36 in) wide lightweight pink cotton fabric

Tracing paper

Fine paintbrush

Light green and pale pink fabric paint

40 cm (16 in) scallop-shaped lace

Dressmaking pins

Cream and pink thread

Sewing needle

Toy filling

Handful of dried lavender

(6)

variation

rose pillow

Cut the pillow from lightweight lilac cotton fabric. Sew purple and gold ribbon diagonally across two corners of one rectangle. Following the template on page 120, paint a cream rose bud on the pillow. Fix the paint by ironing, as before, and make up the cushion when the paint has dried, pouring in a handful of fragrant dried rose buds (these can also aid sleep). Apply a touch of gold glitter paint to the flower.

(5) Pin the rectangles together with the right sides facing (painted side inside). Thread up the needle with the pink thread, knot the end and sew along the outer edges to stitch the layers together, using running stitch. Leave an opening on the lower edge. Remove the pins.

(6) Turn the pillow inside out through the opening in the lower edge so the painted side is on the outside. Fill the pillow with the toy filling by stuffing it through the opening on the lower edge. Pour a handful of lavender into the front of the pillow. Sew the opening closed.

tips

★ After sewing, carefully cut across the seam allowance on the corners; this helps the fabric to lie neatly when you turn it to the right side.

★ Try not to make the stitches too long or the lavender may slip between them and escape from the pillow.

novelty soaps

ages 8–10 years

No one will believe these pretty heart soaps are homemade. If you can't source a heart-shaped flexible ice tray at a local hardware or homeware store, choose one in the shape of stars or even penguins!

(**1**) Place the soap in the top of the double boiler or into the bowl on top of the saucepan filled with a little hot water. (An adult should be at hand to supervise). Heat the boiler or bring the water in the pan to the boil and watch as the soap melts. Turn off the heat.

(**2**) Put on the gloves and add a few drops of the red cosmetic colour, stirring it in with the wooden spoon.

3 Carefully pour the melted soap into the moulds of the flexible ice tray (an adult should do this).

(**4**) Leave the soaps to harden for about two hours, then turn them out of the ice tray.

5 Nestle the soaps in a small basket lined with crumpled cellophane.

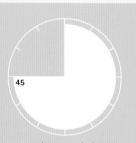

**time needed
45 minutes**
(excluding hardening time)

what you need

200 g (7 oz)
   glycerine soap

Double boiler or
   heatproof bowl and
   saucepan (the bowl
   should sit snugly
   on top)

Thin protective gloves

Red cosmetic colouring

Wooden spoon

Flexible heart-shaped
   ice tray or other
   novelty shape

Small basket

Sheet of cellophane

(4)

variation

string of star soaps

Make deep blue and light blue star-shaped soaps in a flexible star-shaped ice tray. When the surface has hardened (but the soaps aren't hard all the way through), make a hole through the centre of each star. Leave the soaps to harden completely, then thread a double length of narrow ribbon through the holes, leaving a loop at the top and making a knot between each star.

tips

★ Cosmetic colouring is available from craft shops and soap-making websites, but if you can't find it easily, substitute a few drops of food colouring to colour the soaps.

★ When working with cosmetic dyes, wash your hands well with soap and water after finishing the project.

tussie mussie

ages 4–6 years

In ancient times, posies of sweet-smelling herbs called tussie mussies were often carried to hide nasty smells. But they are attractive in their own right, too. This tussie mussie is framed by a delicate paper doily and it makes a beautifully scented bouquet that would be a lovely gift to give to mum on Mother's Day morning.

1 Fold the doily lightly into quarters, pinching the folds at the centre. Cut a small hole at the centre with the scissors.

2 Bunch together the sprigs of rosemary and thyme. Add the sprigs of dill and parsley around the outside to make a pretty posy.

3 Fasten the elastic band around the stems to secure them, making sure the herbs are held tightly together.

4 Slip the stalks carefully down through the hole in the doily so that the lacy part of the doily frames the greenery nicely.

5 Bunch together a few lengths of raffia and tie them in a bow around the tussie mussie beneath the doily. As well as looking pretty, this stops the doily falling off.

45

time needed
45 minutes

what you need

White doily

Scissors

Sprigs of rosemary, thyme, dill and parsley

Elastic band

Orange raffia

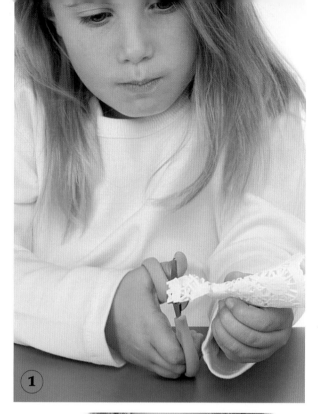

1

2

(5)

tip

★ If you are not presenting the tussie mussie immediately, dampen some kitchen paper and wrap it around the stems then wrap securely in clingfilm.

variation

bouquet garni

Keen cooks will welcome this gift to add flavour to their cooking. Bunch together a few stalks of parsley, a sprig of thyme and a bay leaf, then tie together at the stalks with string ready to throw into a casserole or soup.

lip balm

ages 6–8 years

A luscious pot of vanilla-scented lip balm will be much appreciated by mum, an auntie or another favourite grown-up for keeping lips smooth and glossy. Decorate the tiny container with a shiny sticker and curly ribbon to make it even more special for Mother's Day or for a birthday.

1 Put on the gloves and spoon the petroleum jelly and a little of the lipstick (if using) into the bowl. Add 2–3 drops of the vanilla essence.

2 Mix the ingredients together by mashing them with the back of the spoon until they are blended smoothly.

3 Spoon the balm into the small pot. Screw the lid on tight and wipe away any sticky mess from the pot or lid using a clean kitchen towel or sponge.

4 Stick the heart-shaped sticker on the top of the pot's lid. Tie gift-wrapping ribbon around the outside of the lid. Starting at the knot, pull each end of the ribbon along the blade of a blunt knife to curl it. (An adult might need to help.) If it doesn't curl the first time, try again, keeping the ribbon taut on the blade of the knife all the way along.

**time needed
1 hour**

what you need

Thin protective gloves

2 dessert spoons of petroleum jelly (Vaseline)

New lipstick (optional)

Mixing bowl

Vanilla essence

Spoon

Small pot with lid

Clean kitchen towel or sponge

Heart-shaped sticker

Silver curling gift-wrapping ribbon

Blunt knife

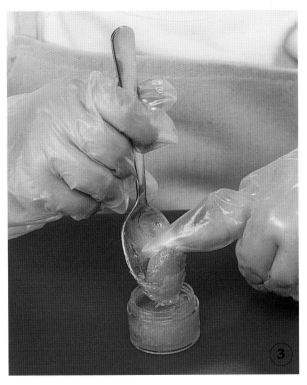

3

tip

★ Thin protective gloves are needed when making the lip balm because it's quite a messy job.

variation

glitter pots

Mini preserve jars make excellent containers for lip balm. After washing the pots and lids well (preferably in a dishwasher, leaving them inside until cool and dry), decorate them with stickers and glitter paint.

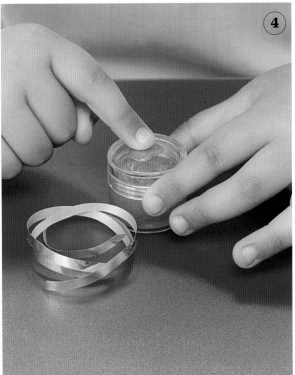

4

CAUTION Don't use old lipstick for this – it might contain germs.

sugar scrub

ages 4–6 years

This fragrant skin scrub for a mum or aunt leaves skin silky smooth and glowing and is the perfect gift for someone special who deserves a little pampering at bathtime. It's especially good for sloughing off rough skin on elbows and heels. Make sure you give this gift to a grown-up only.

(1) Mix together the sugar and olive oil in the bowl to make a gloopy mixture. Stir in the almond essence.

(2) Carefully spoon the mixture into the air-tight pot and screw on the lid. Wipe away any spilt mixture on the pot with a clean cloth.

3 Write a special message on the gift tag. Thread the gift tag onto a length of the gift-wrapping ribbon.

(4) Ask an adult to pull the blunt blade of the knife along each end of the ribbon to curl it. Finally, tie the ribbon with a knot around the lid of the pot.

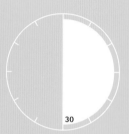

30

time needed
30 minutes

what you need

70 g (2¾ oz) granulated sugar

2 dessert spoons olive oil

Mixing bowl

½ teaspoon almond essence

Small air-tight pot with lid

Clean cloth

Pen

Gift tag

Gift-wrapping ribbon

Blunt knife

(4)

tip

★ Tell the recipient to rub the sugar scrub gently over damp skin, then rinse off with plenty of warm water. Do not use on the face. You could write these instructions on the gift tag in your best writing.

variation

fragrant bath bag

Place a tablespoon of fine oatmeal and a handful each of dried thyme and lavender in the centre of an 18 cm (7¼ in) circle of muslin cut with zig-zag scissors. Gather up the outer edges of the circle and tie them with a length of ribbon. As the water runs through the muslin, it carries the lovely fragrance into the water, while the oatmeal makes the water silky soft. Only give this gift to an adult, and do not give to pregnant women.

floral garden gifts

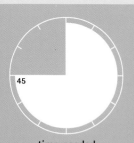

pebble pets

ages 5–6 years

Make this sweet-looking panda for a favourite friend, who's sure to treasure it. All you have to do is paint a nice, round pebble to make the pet, then glue on some funny joggle eyes.

1 Paint the pebble white all over using the large paintbrush. Leave to dry.

2 Paint a black band around the middle of the pebble to make the body.

3 Still using the black paint but with the medium paintbrush, paint patches for the nose and eyes, then the ears. Leave to dry.

4 Glue the joggle eyes onto the eye patches. Set aside until the glue is dry. Draw in a smile with the pink felt-tipped pen.

time needed
45 minutes
(excluding drying time)

what you need

Large pebble

White and black acrylic paint

Large and medium paintbrushes

All-purpose household glue

2 joggle eyes

Pink felt-tipped pen

2

3

4

variations

lion

Choose a large pebble, paint it pale orange and leave to dry. Draw on nose, mouth, eyes and whisker dots with a black waterproof pen. Then paint the mane in stripes of yellow and bright orange paint. Plait lengths of orange wool and make a knot at the end. Glue the plait beneath the lion for a tail.

mouse

Paint a tiny pebble light pink and leave to dry. Dot on eyes with a black waterproof pen. Paint the ears in a deeper pink using a smaller paintbrush. Stick on a tiny red pompom for the nose. Finally, glue a length of plastic thong beneath the mouse for a tail.

rabbit

Paint a pebble grey and leave to dry. Paint on rabbit ears using pink paint and a smaller brush. Draw a nose and mouth using pink and black waterproof pens. Glue joggle eyes above the nose and stick on a white pompom tail.

tip

★ Large painted pebbles make ideal paper-weights.

what you need

3 small cacti

Bowl with drainage
  holes in the bottom

Handfuls of tiny stones

Spoon

Cactus compost

Green-coloured gravel

Blue mosaic squares

cacti garden

ages 4–6 years

Create a colourful indoor garden that will look great on a sunny windowsill with some spiky cacti plants. Be careful of any prickly spines while you are working – you might like to wear gardening gloves to protect your hands.

1 Place the plants in the kitchen sink and water them. Wait for the water to drain away fully before taking them out of the sink.

2 Fill the bottom of the bowl with the small stones to make a drainage layer. Spoon a layer of cactus compost on top.

3 Carefully remove the cacti from their pots and plant them in the bowl. Add more compost around each cactus and press it down firmly with your fingers. Be careful not to fill the bowl right to the top with compost.

4 Spoon the coloured gravel around the cacti to cover the compost.

5 Clear a space among the gravel and press down a mosaic square. Repeat to make a 'path' of mosaic squares around the bowl.

(4)

(5)

variation

planted pot

Water the plant well. Place a layer of stones and a layer of compost in the bottom of an attractive pot, then transfer the plant. Fill in around the sides and top with compost, pressing it down well. Water the plant, then finish off by sticking some artificial butterflies on wires into the earth around the plant.

tip

★ Many cacti are very prickly. If you're not wearing gloves, gently hold a prickly cactus with a few folded sheets of kitchen paper when planting.

1½

**time needed
1½ hours**

what you need

Ruler

Scissors

Strong thread

Coloured plastic beads

15 cm (6 in) thin wire

Plastic drinking straws

Fabric flowers

Wooden batten

Acrylic paint to
   complement the
   flowers

Large paintbrush

flower
curtain

ages 7–8 years

This fantastic curtain of flower petals
looks pretty hung at a window or
doorway. The long 'beads' between
the flowers are actually slices cut from
drinking straws. As a variation, you
can make a mobile by threading flower
petals between stripey straw slices and
crystal beads. Buy silk-look fabric flowers
from florists and craft shops or very
cheaply in discount homeware stores.

1 Cut the thread so it is double the length
you want the bead curtain to hang plus 40 cm
(16 in). (An adult should help here.) Thread
one bead onto the thread. Adjust the bead so
that it sits in the middle of the thread.

2 Bend the wire in half and twist the ends
together to make a 'needle'. Thread both ends
of the thread through the needle.

3 Cut the drinking straws into slices 5 cm
(2 in) in length. Thread one straw slice onto
the thread.

4 Pull apart the silk flowers, separating
them into separate blooms. Each one should
have a tiny hole for threading at the centre.
Thread two flowers onto the thread.

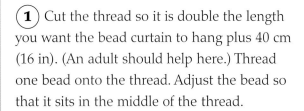

(8)

5 Thread on a bead. Continue threading on straw slices, flowers and beads until you have filled the thread. Make sure you leave enough thread at the top to tie around the batten.

6 Cut more thread and make as many flower strings as you require.

7 Paint the wooden batten in a shade that complements the flowers, and leave to dry.

(8) Tie one end of each flower string to the batten, spaced at equal distances apart. To suspend, screw the batten into the window frame or hang it on a hook placed each side of the window.

tip
★ Glue the threads at the top of each flower string to the back of the curtain batten to keep them secure.

variation

flower mobile

Make up flower strings as before, then tie them to the ends of two mobile wires. Tie the wires together at the centre to form a cross. Hang the mobile on a length of strong thread, threading it with a few petals and beads.

painted plant pot

ages 3–4 years

Here is an excellent gift for garden lovers – a plant pot painted in lively colours then stamped with a bold flower design. Choose the colours for the pot to suit the gardener's own preferences. You can buy ready-made flower stamps from craft and stationery shops. Present your gift filled with a favourite plant or a pot of herbs.

1 Paint the plant pot lavender blue on the outside using the large paintbrush. Using the same colour, paint inside the pot at the top. Leave to dry.

2 Use the medium paintbrush to apply yellow paint to the flower motif on the rubber stamp. Don't put on too much paint or the outline of the flower will come out smudged.

3 Stamp the flower carefully but firmly onto each side of the plant pot. Set aside to dry.

4 Dot orange paint onto the centre of the flower and allow to dry before using the pot.

**time needed
1½ hours**
(excluding drying time)

what you need

- Square terracotta plant pot
- Lavender blue, yellow and orange acrylic paint
- Large and fine paintbrushes
- Large flower rubber stamp

1

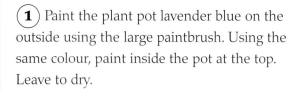

2

3

variations

yellow spattered pot

Paint a terracotta pot yellow all over, including on the inner edge. Leave to dry. Cover your work table and surrounding area with plenty of old newspaper and put on an apron or old shirt, then use an old toothbrush to spatter paint in contrasting colours all over the outside of the pot. Leave to dry. Wash your hands well after spattering.

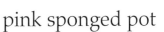

tip

★ You can make your own stamp by cutting a shape from neoprene foam. Glue it to a piece of thick card then paint the foam ready for stamping.

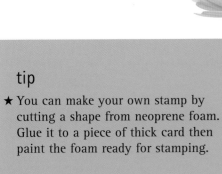

pink sponged pot

This time, paint a terracotta plant pot pale pink all over, then leave to dry. Dab deep pink paint over the outside of the pot using a sponge. Leave to dry, then paint the rim of the pot aquamarine.

bird feeder

ages 8–10 years

Hang a birdfeeder in a garden and just watch the birds flock in. This makes a perfect present for a nature lover. Why not wrap up a bird-spotting book with it so the recipient can enjoy recognizing the different species?

1 Measure the circumference of one plastic lid. Use a pair of metal cutters to cut a rectangle of wire mesh 18 cm (7¼ in) high and 2 cm (¾ in) longer than the circumference of the lid.

2 Using the needle, make a row of holes around the edge of one of the plastic lids; this will be the base. (An adult might need to help younger children with this task.)

(3) Bend the mesh into a cylinder, overlapping the ends. Stand the cylinder upright inside the base. Starting at the overlap, oversew the bottom of the mesh to the base by sewing through the holes in the mesh then the holes in the base with fine wire, pulling the wire tight after each hole. When you have worked all the way around, twist the ends of the wire together.

(4) Oversew the overlapped edges of the mesh together.

time needed
2 hours

what you need

Ruler

2 plastic lids of the same size

Metal cutters

Wire mesh

Thick needle

Fine wire

Purple wire

8 assorted purple and pink beads

Small pair of pliers

Packet of peanuts

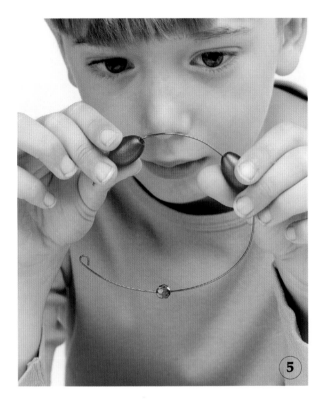

variation

nightlight holder

Thread beads onto coloured wire, then wrap the wire tightly around the rim of a preserve jar. Twist the ends of the wire securely together. Make a beaded handle, as before, and hook the ends onto the wire on either side of the jar. Place a nightlight inside.

(5) Snip a 25 cm (10 in) length of purple wire to make a handle. Bend one end into a loop with the pliers. Thread four beads onto each end of the handle. Make a loop at the other end of the handle. Hook the looped ends onto each side of the top of the wire feeder.

6 Pour in the peanuts and place the other lid on top of the feeder.

tip
★ Hang the feeder high up where cats and other animals cannot reach it.

CAUTION Be very careful with lit candles. For safety, always ask an adult to light the candle and never leave a lit candle burning unattended.

paper daffodils

ages 6–8 years

This delightful bouquet of paper daffodils is an ideal springtime gift. As a finishing touch, present the flowers with some vibrant green paper leaves wrapped in colourful tissue paper.

1 For each flower trumpet cut a 6 x 4.5 cm (2½ x 1¾ in) rectangle of yellow crepe paper, cutting the short edges parallel with the lines on the paper. Gently stretch one long edge between your fingers.

2 Glue the short edges together to form a trumpet-shaped tube. Cut off the top of a green bendy drinking straw 2 cm (¾ in) above the bend. Dab glue inside the bottom of the trumpet. Slip the top of the straw into the trumpet and squeeze the bottom of the trumpet around the straw.

3 Trace the petal template on page 121 then transfer the design six times onto the yellow crepe paper, matching the arrow on the template to the direction of the lines on the paper. Cut out the petals. Glue the bottom of three petals around the trumpet. Glue the other petals in the gaps. Leave the glue to dry, then open out the petals. Bend the top of the straw 'stalk' forward.

time needed
1 hour

what you need

Ruler

Pencil

Scissors

Yellow crepe paper

All-purpose household glue

4 green bendy plastic drinking straws

Mid-green paper

Clear sticky tape

Light green tissue paper

Organza ribbon

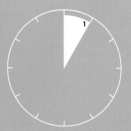

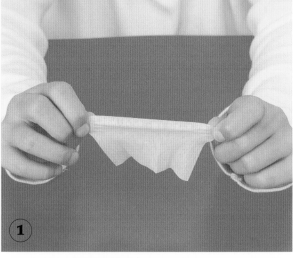

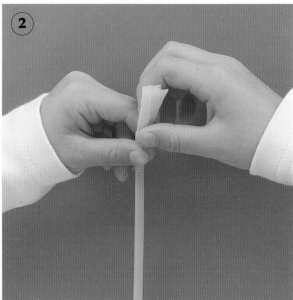

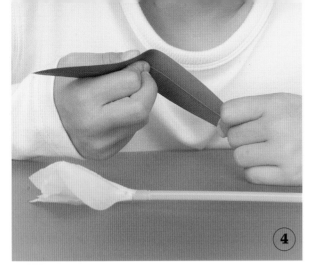

(4)

(4) Using the leaf template on page 121, cut a leaf from the mid-green paper. Fold the leaf along the centre, then open it out flat again. Gently pull the tip of the leaf between thumb and finger to curve the leaf tip backward.

5 Repeat the steps to make four daffodils and four leaves. To make a pretty bouquet, bunch the daffodils and leaves together and bind them in position with clear sticky tape.

6 Wrap the flowers and leaves in a piece of light green tissue paper. Tie this gift wrap in place with a length of organza ribbon.

variations

purple fringed flower

Cut a 6 x 4 cm (2½ x 1½ in) rectangle of pale pink crepe paper. Cut one long edge into a fringe. Glue the other long edge around the top of the straw. Make six petals from purple crepe paper and glue them around the straw.

cerise feather flower

Glue yellow feathers into the top of a straw. Make six petals from bright pink crepe paper and glue them around the straw.

fringed feather flower

Glue green feathers into the top of a straw. Cut a 45 x 6 cm (18 x 2½ in) strip of pale pink crepe paper. Cut one long edge into a fringe. Glue the other long edge around the top of the straw.

tip
★ Gently push your thumb into the crepe paper trumpet to open out the shape.

chopstick wind chimes

ages 6–7 years

Let these stripey wind chimes tinkle in the breeze by hanging them in the garden or indoors by an open window.

(1) Paint six chopsticks in stripes using shades of blue, turquoise, purple and lilac. Wash and dry the paintbrush between each colour. Insert the chopsticks into a piece of plastic clay to dry.

(2) Cut six equal lengths of narrow braid. Tie one length around the top of each chopstick. Fix them in place with a dab of glue.

3 Use the large needle to make six holes around the edge of the plastic lid. (An adult might like to help at this stage.)

(4) Thread the braid from one chopstick up through one hole. Knot the braid on top of the lid. Fix all the chopsticks to the lid in the same way, making sure that they hang down at the same level.

5 Make a hole in the centre of the lid with the needle. To hang the chimes, thread another length of narrow braid through the hole and knot it beneath the lid.

**time needed
2 hours**

what you need

6 chopsticks

Blue, turquoise, purple and lilac acrylic paint

Medium paintbrush

Plastic clay

Narrow braid

Scissors

PVA glue

Large needle

Plastic lid from snack tube

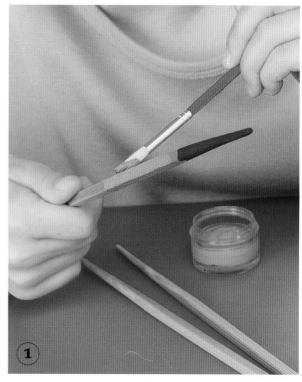

①

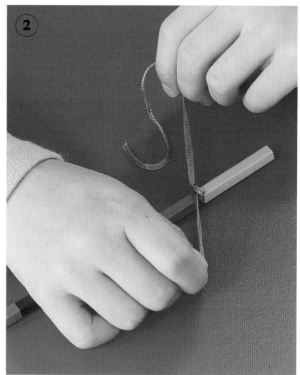

②

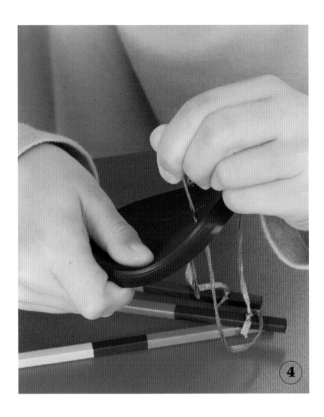

variation

bead mobile

Cut six equal lengths of ribbon. Thread a bead onto the centre of each length. Thread both ends through multicoloured beads (keep the colours random). Punch six holes around the edge of a plastic snack tube top and thread both ends of the ribbons through each hole, knotting as before. Suspend from a ribbon fixed to a hole in the centre of the lid, as before.

tip
★ Dab glue on the knots to hold them in place.

pressed-flower box

ages 8–10 years

Collecting and pressing flowers and leaves is a great hobby, especially if you use them to make gifts like this sweet box. It would be a lovely present to give on Mother's Day, filled with yummy edible treats (see pages 104–119).

1 Paint the outside of the box and lid with lilac paint. Leave to dry, then paint the inside of the box red.

2 Hold a pressed yellow flower with a pair of tweezers. Spread a little glue over the back of the flower with the cocktail stick, then stick the flower on the centre of the lid.

(3) Glue three red pressed flowers around the edge of the lid, then stick three white flowers between them, using the tweezers and cocktail stick as before.

(4) Glue single red and purple petals around the rim of the lid using the tweezers and cocktail stick as before. Leave to dry.

(5) Put the lid on the box. Glue pairs of leaves around the side of the box using the tweezers and cocktail stick as before.

2

**time needed
2 hours**
(excluding drying time)

what you need

Small box with lid

Lilac and red
  acrylic paint

Large paintbrush

Assorted pressed flowers
  and leaves

Pair of tweezers

PVA glue

Cocktail stick

(3)

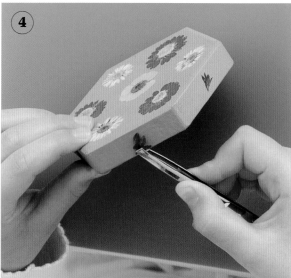

(4)

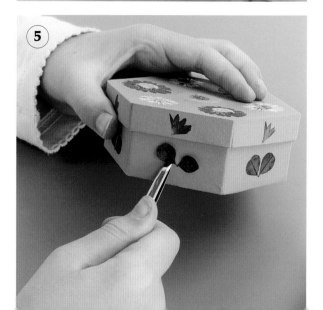

(5)

variations

pressed-flower picture

Tear strips of coloured, textured paper and stick them to a piece of white paper. Glue pressed flowers and flower-shaped stickers in rows to the torn strips of paper. Place the picture in a frame. Decorate the frame with flower-shaped stickers.

mirror frame

Glue pressed rose buds on stems to the frame surrounding a mirror. Leave to dry on a flat surface before hanging on the wall.

tips

★ To press flowers, place picked garden flower heads on one side of a piece of blotting paper. Fold the blotting paper over the top of the flowers. Press the flowers between the pages of a heavy book or in a flower press. Carefully remove the flowers after a few weeks.

★ Coat the box and its lid with PVA glue once you have placed all the flowers to seal them in place.

shell
mobile

ages 6–7 years

Shells look lovely hanging in the garden. Suspend some on coloured yarn to hang from a driftwood stick for a mobile that will withstand sun, wind and rain. You can buy shells ready drilled for craftwork from craft shops, or go beachcombing for shells with natural holes.

1 Cut three equal lengths of yarn. Thread one of the shells with one hole onto the end of one length of yarn. Tie the shell to the yarn.

2 Make a big knot about 2.5 cm (1 in) above the shell. Thread the yarn in and out of the holes on one of the shells with two holes. Make a big knot on top of the shell.

3 Thread on three more shells with two holes in the same way, making big knots on each side of the shells. Tie the string of shells to hang from the middle of the driftwood stick.

4 Make two more strings of shells in the same way and tie them to the stick on either side of the first string.

**time needed
1 hour**

what you need

Coloured yarn

3 shells with 1 drilled hole

12 shells with 2 drilled holes

Driftwood stick

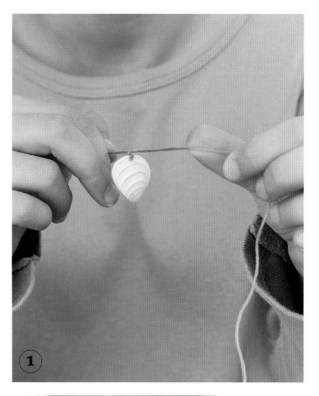

1

2

variation

shell picture

Glue shells to a piece of yellow card. Fix the card in a box frame deep enough for the 3D picture.

5 Knot three new lengths of yarn together 10 cm (4 in) from one end. Plait the yarns until the plait is 21 cm (8½ in) long. Make a knot. Tie the free ends of the plait to each end of the stick to suspend it. Cut off the extra yarn.

tip

★ Paint the shells in cheerful colours if you'd prefer a bright look to your picture.

accessories

button key-ring

ages 4–6 years

We all know people who are always losing their keys. This bright, chunky key-ring is just the answer. To make it, you need to collect together lots of odd buttons in different vibrant colours to thread onto a length of fine cord.

1 Fold the fine cord in half. Make a knot about 2.5 cm (1 in) in from the fold.

2 Thread the buttons onto the cord by pushing each end of the cord through one of the holes in the buttons. Choose the buttons so you get a random selection of colours and textures.

3 When you have threaded on the last button, knot the ends of the cord together tightly beneath it. Cut off the excess cord.

4 Slip the loop of the cord onto the key-ring (an adult might need to help).

time needed
20 minutes

what you need

30 cm (12 in) fine cord

10 coloured buttons

Key-ring

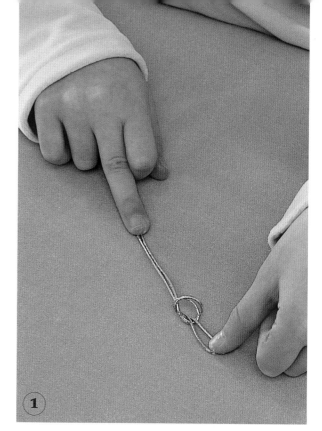

1

2

(3)

variations

bead key-ring

Instead of using buttons to make the key-ring, thread beads onto the cord. Make sure the beads are chunky and choose cord and beads in matching colour tones.

felt flower key-ring

Trace the flower template on page 121, then transfer the design onto thin card. Cut out the shape and draw around it six times on distinct bright colours of felt or in different shades of the same colour. Cut out the flowers. Make a hole through the centre of each and thread them onto the key-ring cord as before.

tip
★ Dab the ends of the cord with glue to stop them unravelling.

ribbon key-ring

Knot different-coloured ribbon directly to the key-ring. Make sure the pieces of ribbon are all about the same length and cut the ends of the ribbons at a slant.

jewelled hair clasp

ages 6–8 years

Here is a very sparkly gift for someone special, whether it's a best friend or a glamourous granny. It combines brightly-coloured feathers with deep jewel-coloured craft stones (buy them from specialist craft stores or websites). Choose dyed feathers from a craft shop or look for fallen feathers when you are out for a walk. Jewellery stones come in all sorts of shapes and colours and are especially fun to work with when you want to make gifts look really special.

(1) Glue the coloured feather so that it pokes outward on the end of the hair clasp.

(2) Glue one of the jewellery stones on top of the feather.

(3) Continue gluing jewellery stones along the length of the hair clasp until you have a look you like. Set the hair clasp aside while the glue dries.

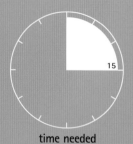

time needed
15 minutes

what you need

All-purpose household glue

Coloured feather

Metal hair clasp

Round jewellery stones

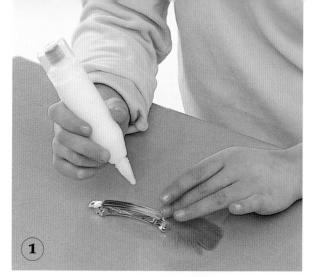
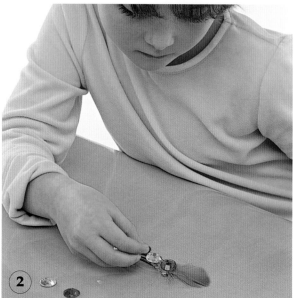
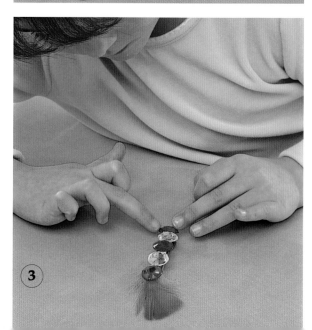

variations

use your imagination

Make all sorts of arrangements of feathers and jewellery stones on a hair clasp. Alternatively, leave out the feathers and simply glue colourful square jewellery stones in a row along the clasp. Leave to set before wearing.

tips

★ If the feathers seem too long, simply cut them to the length you want.

★ Beware of using too much glue, or it will show on the finished clasp.

★ Leave the glue to dry for a few hours before handling the hair clasps.

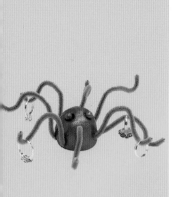

octopus ring holder

ages 3–4 years

Luckily, this amusing octopus has enough legs to hold lots of jewellery. He is made from air-drying clay and his bendy legs are pipecleaners. An older sister might like him as a present.

(1) Roll a 5 cm (2 in) wide ball of clay between your palms to make the octopus body. Rest the octopus on your work surface. Press the beads into the top of the octopus to dent the clay at the top, where his eyes should be. Remove the beads.

(2) Cut the pipecleaners into eight 12 cm (4¾ in) lengths for the legs. Push the legs into the octopus toward the bottom of his body, four on each side, then remove them. Set the octopus aside to harden.

(3) Paint the octopus with the aquamarine paint. Leave to dry, then paint over the top with the pearlized paint.

(4) Glue the eyes to the head in the eye holes. Dab glue on the end of each leg and poke them into the holes you made. (An adult might need to help.) Bend the legs in a curve. Set aside until the glue is dry.

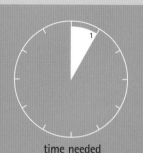

**time needed
1 hour**
(excluding drying time)

what you need

Air-drying clay

2 beads

4 lilac pipecleaners

Aquamarine and pearlized green acrylic paint

Large paintbrush

All-purpose household glue

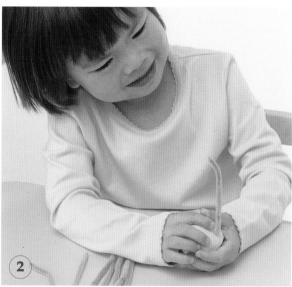

(4)

variations

striped insect

Roll a 5 cm (2 in) wide ball of clay into an oval shape for this exotic insect. Press two beads into one end to dent the clay. Remove the beads. Cut white pipecleaners into six 12 cm (4 ¾ in) lengths for the legs. Push three legs into each side of the insect, then remove them. Leave the clay to harden, then paint the insect in stripes. Glue the bead eyes and pipecleaner legs in place.

tips

★ The insects can also be used for hanging earrings on.

★ Make sure you cover the work surface before you get out the clay and paint.

★ You can recycle coloured plastic packaging to make insect wings.

blue insect

Make the insect body as above, pressing in and taking out the beads and legs. Using the template on page 123, cut two wings from green plastic, then make two slits on the top of the body using the wings. Remove the wings. Leave the clay to harden overnight. Paint the insect with blue pearlized paint. Glue the bead eyes and yellow chenille pipecleaner legs in place, bending them up. Glue the wings into the slits.

jeans party bag

ages 8–10 years

Recycle a pocket from an old pair of jeans that you have grown out of to make a fantastic party bag for a friend's birthday. If you make two bags from one pair of jeans, you can keep one for yourself. Decorate the bag with glitter paint and sparkling jewellery stones.

1 Carefully cut out one back pocket from the jeans. (An adult may need to help if the denim is very thick.)

2 Paint a line of pink glitter paint along the outer edges of the pocket by squeezing it from the bottle. The glitter paint stops the fabric fraying. Paint along the top edge of the pocket, then leave to dry.

3 Turn the pocket over and paint the top edge on the wrong side of the jeans too. Leave the pocket to dry.

4 Glue the jewellery stones in a row across the front of the pocket. Glue two of the heart-shaped jewellery stones above and two below the squares.

1½

time needed
1½ hours
(excluding drying time)

what you need

Scissors

Old pair of jeans

Pink glitter paint in easy-application squeeze bottle

All-purpose household glue

3 square jewellery stones

4 heart-shaped jewellery stones

Sewing needle

Blue sewing thread

90 cm (3 ft) each of pink, purple and red cord

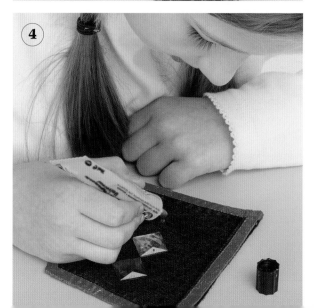

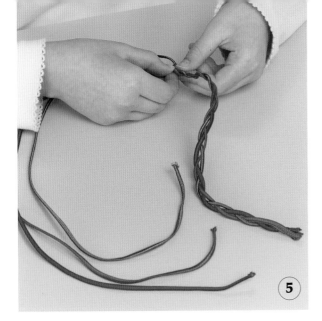

(5) To make the handle, thread the needle with blue thread. Sew one end of the lengths of pink, purple and red cord together. Plait the cords, then sew the other ends together. Sew the ends of the cords inside the side edges of the pocket.

tips

★ You might need to use adult jeans for a larger bag. Don't forget to ask permission first!

★ Rest the pocket on an old plastic carrier bag when applying glitter paint so you don't spoil your work surface.

variations

flower purse

Cut a small pocket out of an old shirt (choose one with a button fastening. Paint the edges with gold glitter paint and the button with purple glitter paint. Glue a few flower-shaped sequins to the front.

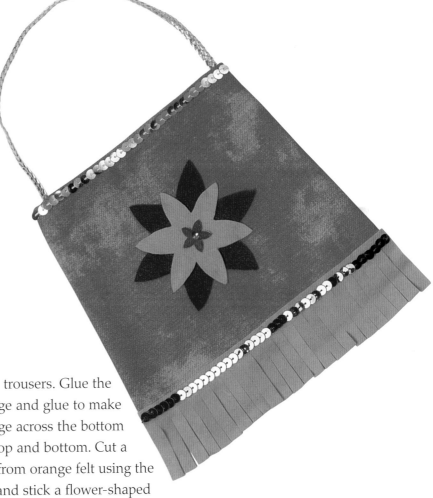

fringed handbag

Cut the bottom off one leg of a pair of old colourful trousers. Glue the hem together to make a bag. Turn under the top edge and glue to make a top hem. Stick a strip of orange felt cut into a fringe across the bottom of the bag, then add a string of sequins across the top and bottom. Cut a large flower out of purple felt and a smaller flower from orange felt using the template on page 121. Glue the flowers to the bag and stick a flower-shaped sequin on top. Sew a gold braid handle inside the sides of the top of the bag.

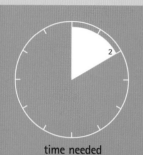

what you need

Tape measure

Pencil

Scissors

23 cm (9 in) square
turquoise felt

23 cm (9 in) square
pink fleece

Sewing needle

Purple sewing thread

35 cm (14 in) string of
purple sequins

Four flower-shaped
sequins

Pink embroidery thread

Embroidery needle

Dressmaking pins

felt glasses case

ages 6–8 years

Decorate this elegant glasses case with lots of shiny sequins. The soft case is padded with a fluffy fleece lining to protect the glasses inside. It's a perfect gift for people who wear glasses, or for a friend who's going on holiday with a new pair of shades.

1 Cut two 20 x 10 cm (8 x 4 in) rectangles of turquoise felt and pink fleece for the case.

2 Thread the needle with the purple thread and sew the sequin string in a squiggle along one of the felt rectangles.

3 Thread the embroidery needle with one strand of pink embroidery thread. (An adult might need to help at this stage.) Sew the flower-shaped sequins at random along the sequin string.

4 Pin each felt rectangle onto one of the fleece rectangles. Thread the embroidery needle with three strands of pink embroidery thread. Using running stitch (see page 21), sew the layers together along the top, short edge. Remove the pins.

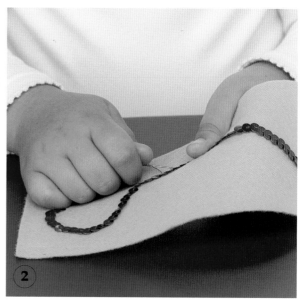

(5)

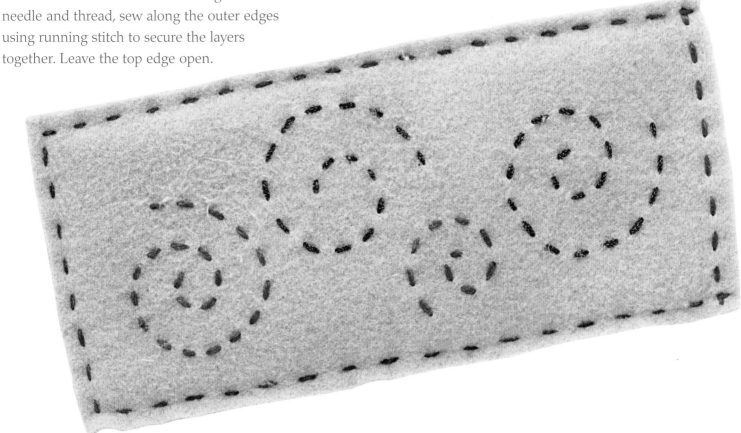

tip

★ Glue the threads of the sequin string to the back of the sequins to stop them unravelling, but be careful not to use too much glue.

variation

spiral design

In step 2 sew spirals in running stitch using alternately embroidery thread and glittery yarn. Subsitute turquoise fleece for the padding.

(5) Pin both rectangles together, making sure the felt is on the outside. Using the same needle and thread, sew along the outer edges using running stitch to secure the layers together. Leave the top edge open.

bangle bag

ages 6–8 years

This gorgeous bag has bangles for handles so it can be worn around the wrist to a special party or hung at home as a jewellery store. The bag looks best made from silky fabric: choose one to match a favourite party dress, perhaps. As an extra gift you could place some more bangles in the bag for the lucky recipient to wear on her other wrist.

1 Cut two 16 cm (6½ in) squares of fabric with the zig-zag scissors. Pin the squares together with the right sides facing each other. Thread up the needle and, using running stitch (see page 21), sew around three of the outer edges. Start halfway down one side and finish halfway up the opposite side. Remove the pins.

2 Fold over the side edges above the stitching and glue them down. Turn the bag right side out.

3 Fold under 2.5 cm (1 in) of fabric on the top edge of one side of the bag. Pin a bangle under the fold. Sew below the fold to enclose the bangle, removing the pins to gather up the thread as you sew. Attach the second bangle to the other side of the bag in the same way.

1½

**time needed
1½ hours**

what you need

Tape measure

Pencil

Zig-zag scissors

20 cm (8 in) of 90 cm (36 in) wide silky fabric

Dressmaking pins

Sewing needle

Matching sewing thread

Fabric glue

2 bangles

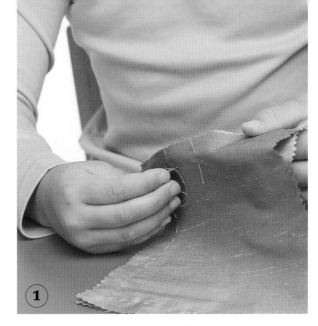

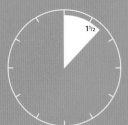

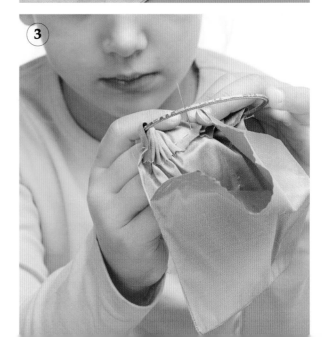

variations

red bag

In step 3, catch in a star-shaped charm when gathering the thread by passing the needle through the loop at the top of the charm. Position the charm to sit in the centre of the gathers.

orange pouch

In step 3, replace the bangles with two equal lengths of matching ribbon. Be careful not to sew in the ribbon as you sew along the fold.

seed bracelet

ages 4–6 years

You can make fabulous jewellery if you collect the seeds from pumpkins and melons. Give the seeds a good wash and dry them well, then paint them and thread onto fine elastic to make this pretty bracelet. To make a necklace, all you need to do is add more seeds.

(1) Paint one side of each seed lilac, aquamarine or lavender blue. Leave them to dry, then turn the seeds over and paint the other side.

(2) Pierce a hole through the middle of the seeds using the thick needle. (An adult may need to help.)

(3) Tie a knot at the end of the jewellery elastic, then thread on the seeds, alternating the colours.

4 When you have threaded on enough seeds to fit around a wrist, knot the ends of the elastic together tightly twice. Cut off the extra elastic.

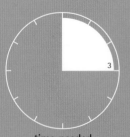

**time needed
3 hours**

what you need

30–35 pumpkin or melon seeds

Lilac, aquamarine and lavender blue acrylic paint

Medium paintbrush

Thick needle

30 cm (12 in) jewellery elastic

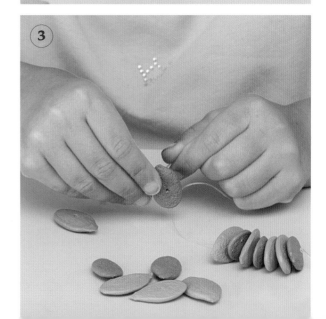

variations

seed necklace

Paint seeds with lavender blue acrylic paint,
leave them to dry, then dot with green paint.
Leave to dry, then repeat on the other side of
each seed. Make a hole through the top of the
seeds and thread them onto a length of green
thonging. Start with a knot, thread on three
seeds, then make another knot. Thread on
another three seeds and make a further knot.
Continue in this way until you reach the
desired length.

seed hair slide

Paint sunflower seeds with purple glitter paint,
leave to dry, then glue onto a hair slide.

tips
★ If you prefer, colour the seeds with waterproof
   felt-tipped pens.

★ Shirring elastic can be used to thread the
   seeds instead of jewellery elastic, if liked.

bath mitt

ages 6–8 years

Here is a luxurious present for someone who deserves to be pampered. It's a bath mitt made from two face flannels and trimmed with colourful beads, lace and ribbon roses. If you are giving this to your mum as a gift, make sure you also give her an hour's peace once a week for maximum enjoyment.

1 Cut a 21 x 16 cm (8½ x 6½ in) rectangle from one of the face flannels, making sure one of the short edges runs along one of the flannel's hemmed edges. Cut the opposite short edge in a curve.

2 In exactly the same way, cut another mitt to match from the second flannel.

③ Pin the bead edging along the bottom of one mitt. Thread up the needle with matching thread, then sew the edging in place using running stitch (see page 21). (An adult might need to help at this stage.) Remove the pins.

④ Pin and sew the length of flower lace across the mitt above the bead edging. Remove the pins.

5 Sew the ribbon roses in a neat row above the flower lace.

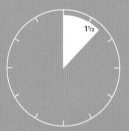

time needed
1½ hours

what you need

Tape measure

Pencil

Scissors

2 face flannels

Dressmaking pins

16 cm (6½ in)
bead edging

Matching sewing
threads

Sewing needle

15 cm (6 in) flower lace

Three ribbon roses

variation

ric-rac mitt

Make the mitt as before but this time using dark blue flannels. Sew rows of ric-rac and flower lace across the centre of one side of the mitt.

6 Pin the mitts together with the right sides facing each other (on the inside). Sew along both sides and the top leaving the bottom edge open. Remove the pins and turn the mitt to the right side.

tips

★ Make the mitt in colours to match the bathroom of the person you are giving it to.

★ Dab glue on the ends of the bead edging to stop the beads falling off.

papier-mâché choker

ages 4–6 years

It's hard to believe that this vibrant papier-mâché choker features beads made from ordinary kitchen paper! After making the beads all you have to do is paint them in bright shades and thread them onto colourful thonging.

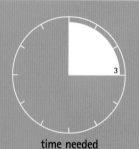

**time needed
3 hours**
(excluding drying time)

what you need

6 sheets of
   kitchen paper

PVA glue

Cocktail sticks

Blue, pink and red
   acrylic paint

Fine paintbrush

Plastic clay

1m (3 ft) red plastic
   thonging

1 Tear the sheets of paper into small pieces and leave them to soak for about an hour in a bowl of PVA glue mixed with a little water (use 1 tablespoon of water to 2 tablespoons PVA).

2 Squeeze pieces of the soaked tissue to release some of the glue and roll into seven balls about 1.5 cm (⅝ in) wide. Put the beads in a warm place for a few hours to dry.

3 When the beads are firm, make a hole through the centre of each one using a cocktail stick. (An adult may need to help.) Gently roll the beads back into shape. Leave overnight to harden completely.

4 Slip the beads onto more cocktail sticks. Paint them blue. Insert the cocktail sticks into a piece of plastic clay and leave to dry.

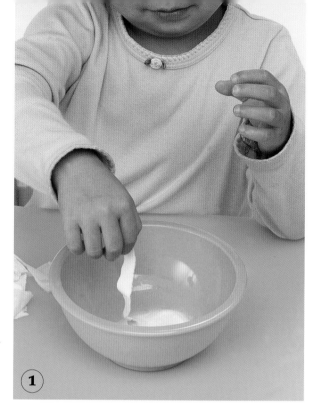

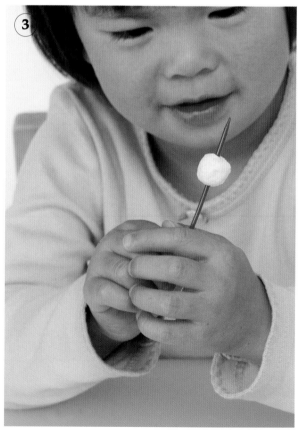

(5) Paint swirls on the beads using the pink and red paint. Leave to dry.

6 Thread the beads onto the plastic thonging, knotting the thong on each side of the beads and cutting off the extra thonging.

variations

bracelet
Paint eight papier-mâché beads pink and thread them onto jewellery elastic, placing a small bead between each one. Tie a knot and cut off the extra elastic.

heart pendant
Make a large papier-mâché ball, as before, then mould it into a heart shape. Make a hole through the top, allow to harden, then paint it red. Leave to dry, then apply pink glitter paint and thread onto a length of lilac cord.

tip
★ Coat the beads with clear nail varnish for protection.

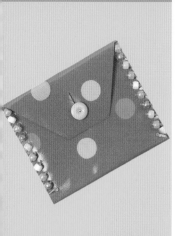

make-up bag

ages 8–10 years

A smart bag to hold make-up is a very practical present that is sure to get plenty of use. This delightful design is trimmed with braid and beads.

1 Cut a 32 x 15 cm (12¾ x 6 in) rectangle of plastic-coated fabric. Cut a slit to match the diameter of the button 2 cm (¾ in) from one short edge of the rectangle. This end of the rectangle will be the bag's flap.

2 Fold up the other end of the bag by 12 cm (4¾ in). Secure the side edges together with paper clips. Draw slanted edges on each side of the flap with the pencil and ruler, then cut out.

3 Fold the flap over the bag and mark the position of the button through the middle of the button hole with the pencil. Open out the bag, thread up the sewing needle and sew the button at the mark.

4 Refold the bag and secure with paper clips again. Thread the large needle with the narrow braid. Oversew the sides of the bag (push the needle through from back to front, pass it around the cut edges to the back and up to the front again), threading a bead onto each stitch. Knot the ends of the braid.

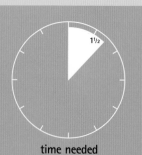

**time needed
1½ hours**

what you need

Tape measure

Pencil

Ruler

Scissors

Plastic-coated fabric

Button

Paper clips

Sewing needle

Matching thread

Large needle

Narrow braid

Beads with large holes

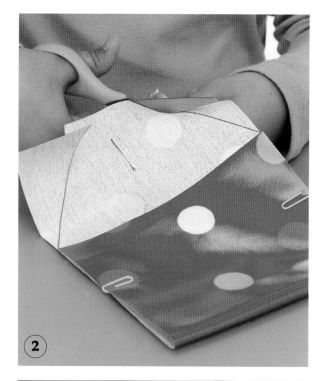

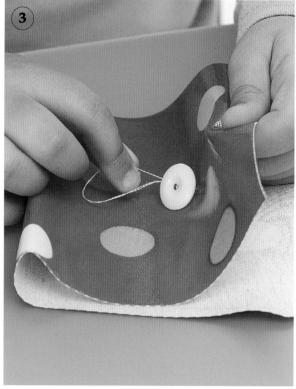

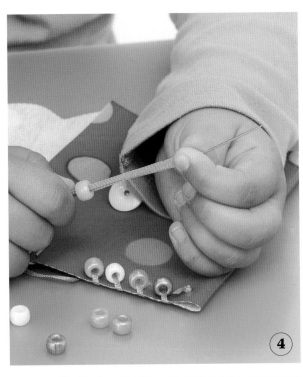

(4)

variations

mirror case

Cut a 19 x 9.5 cm (7¾ x 3¾ in) rectangle of plastic-coated fabric and fold it in half. Sew the edges together with thonging using running stitch (see page 21), threading a heart-shaped bead onto the last stitch at each side. Slip a 7.5 cm (3¼ in) mirror into the case.

tips

★ When sewing, if you find it difficult to make holes with a needle large enough for the narrow braid, carefully make them with the point of a pair of scissors.

★ The beads used here are called pony beads; they have large holes, come in lots of lovely colours and are cheap to buy from craft shops.

comb case

Cut a 16 x 12 cm (6½ x 4¾ in) rectangle of patterned plastic-coated fabric. Fold the rectangle in half lengthways. Sew the edges together with narrow braid using running stitch (see page 21), threading a star-shaped bead onto the last stitch at the top of the case. Slip a comb into the case.

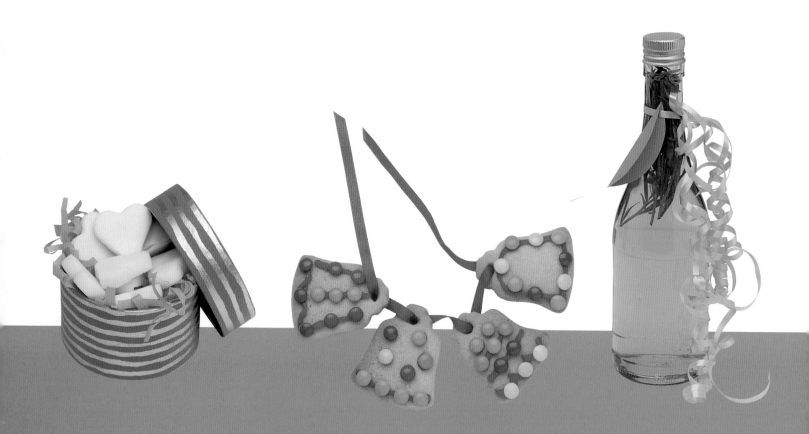

edible treats

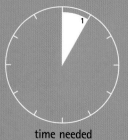

**time needed
1 hour**

what you need

500 g (1 lb) granulated
    sugar

150 ml (¼ pint) milk

Saucepan

Wooden spoon

150 g (5 oz) desiccated
    coconut

2 drops vanilla essence

20 cm (8 in) square
    baking tin or pie
    dish, oiled

Pink food colouring

Blunt knife

Air-tight glass jar

coconut
ice

ages 6–8 years

To make this yummy gift look extra special, display the pastel colours of the coconut ice to best advantage by presenting them in an attractive glass jar tied with matching or contrasting coloured ribbon.

1 Place the sugar and milk in the pan and heat, stirring with the wooden spoon, so that the sugar dissolves. Bring the mixture to the boil and continue cooking for ten minutes. (An adult should supervise at this stage.)

2 Remove the pan from the heat and let the bubbles subside. Stir in the desiccated coconut with the spoon. Add the drops of vanilla essence.

3 Spoon half of the coconut mixture into the baking tin or pie dish, pressing gently with the back of the spoon to even out the surface, if necessary.

4 Stir a few drops of pink food colouring into the remaining mixture to give it a delicate pink colour. Spoon this mixture carefully over the first half of the mixture in the tin and flatten gently with the back of the spoon, if required.

5 Before it is completely cold, cut the coconut ice into pieces using the blunt knife.

6 When the coconut ice is cold, carefully remove the squares and place in the air-tight glass container and secure the lid.

tip
★ Use a cookie cutter to stamp the coconut ice into simple shapes, such as hearts, stars, circles or diamonds.

variation

icy blue coconut ice
In step 4, instead of tinting the ice pink, substitute a few drops of blue food colouring. Once the coconut ice is completely cold, nestle the pieces in a cardboard cone filled with contrasting-coloured shredded tissue paper.

peppermint creams

ages 4–6 years

Make these heart-shaped confections as a romantic gift for Valentine's Day. (Mums and dads will love them.) Make sure you disguise your identity as the sender of the gift to add an extra element of surprise on the big day.

1 Sieve the icing sugar into the bowl. Add the beaten egg white and the water.

2 Stir the mixture to a smooth paste with the spoon, then add the peppermint essence. Be careful not to add more than 2 drops. Set the mixture aside for 10 minutes.

3 Lightly dust a sheet of baking foil with icing sugar. Roll the paste out flat, about 1 cm (½ in) thick.

4 Stamp out heart shapes with the cookie cutter, rerolling the mixture as necessary. Set them aside to dry overnight.

5 Fill the gift box with shredded tissue paper, then place the peppermint creams on top.

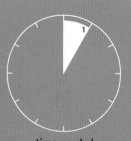

**time needed
1 hour**
(not including drying)

what you need

Sieve

500 g (1 lb) icing sugar, plus extra for dusting

Mixing bowl

1 egg white, beaten

1 tablespoon water

Wooden spoon

2 drops peppermint essence

Baking foil

Rolling pin

Heart-shaped cookie cutter

Gift box

Shredded tissue paper

①

②

variation

disc-shaped creams

Instead of cutting out heart shapes, roll small balls of peppermint-cream mixture and flatten them into disc shapes. Set aside to dry as before, then place in a box.

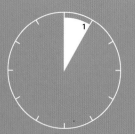

time needed
1 hour
(excluding drying time)

what you need

Sieve

500g (1lb) icing sugar, plus extra for dusting

Mixing bowl

1 egg white, beaten

1 tablespoon water

Wooden spoon

2 drops peppermint essence

1 drop red food colouring

Pastry board

Baking foil

Ribbon

candy canes

ages 4–6 years

Marbled candy canes are a traditional winter festival gift that look good poking out of the top of a Christmas stocking, tied to a tree with ribbon, or adorning a beautifully wrapped present. They are the ideal gift for brothers and sisters.

1 Sieve the sugar into the bowl. Add the beaten egg white and the water.

2 Stir the mixture to a smooth paste with the spoon, then add the peppermint essence. Don't add more than 2 drops.

3 Add the red food colouring. Be careful not to add more than 1 drop. Transfer the mixture onto a pastry board lightly dusted with icing sugar. Gently knead the colour into the mixture, without mixing it in completely – keep the colour looking nice and swirly. Set the paste aside for 10 minutes.

4 Pull off 3 cm (1¼ in) balls of paste and roll on the board into lengths about 1 cm (½ in) thick. Bend over the top of the canes. Set aside on a sheet of baking foil to dry overnight.

5 Tie a length of ribbon around each cane to finish it off.

variation

different-shaped canes

In step 3 knead the paste until the colour has blended in fully, then, in step 4, bend the canes into various shapes.

iced cookies

ages 8–10 years

These tasty biscuits are not just easy to make, they are fun to decorate with ready-made coloured icing. Bake them for a birthday party and let guests customize one each, or stamp them out using Christmas- or Easter-shaped cutters for seasonal celebrations.

1 Place the butter, sugar and golden syrup in the mixing bowl and cream them together with the wooden spoon. Now beat in the egg.

2 Sieve the flour, cinnamon and ginger into the creamed mixture. Stir the mixture, then knead it to a firm dough. Set the dough aside for 40 minutes to rest.

3 Lightly dust the pastry board with flour. Roll the dough out flat, about 5 mm (¼ in) thick. Stamp out lots of star shapes with the star-shaped cutter. Place them on a sheet of nonstick baking paper on a baking sheet.

4 Place the baking sheet in a preheated oven, 160°C (325°F), Gas Mark 3, for 15 minutes. (An adult should assist at this stage.) Remove from the oven and allow to cool on the wire rack.

5 Warm the apricot jam in the small pan and brush onto the centre of a star.

6 Roll a ball of red icing 2 cm (¾ in) in diameter. Flatten the ball between your fingers and press onto the centre of the star. Press coloured sugar pearls into the icing to make circles or other patterns.

7 When the icing has set, place the biscuits in the gift box.

**time needed
1 hour**
(excluding resting and baking)

what you need

75 g (3 oz) butter

75 g (3 oz) granulated sugar

1 rounded tablespoon golden syrup

Mixing bowl

Wooden spoon

1 egg

Sieve

375 g (12 oz) self-raising flour, plus extra for dusting

½ teaspoon ground cinnamon

1 teaspoon ground ginger

Pastry board

Rolling pin

Star-shaped cookie cutter

Nonstick baking paper

Baking sheet

Wire rack

2 tablespoons apricot jam

Small saucepan

Pastry brush

1 pack ready-to-roll red icing

Coloured sugar pearls

Gift box

Tissue paper

1

tip

★ Cover a small box with gift wrap that suits the personality of the person you are giving the biscuits to before arranging them inside.

★ These cookies will keep in a sealed container for one week.

variation

daisy biscuits

Cut out the biscuits using a daisy-shaped cutter. When decorating them, place a circle of green icing at the centre of each biscuit, then press an icing flower in the middle, and decorate with coloured pearl 'petals'.

6

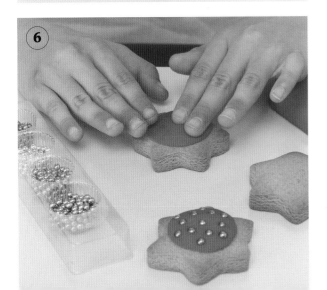

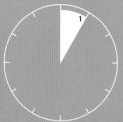

**time needed
1 hour**
(excluding cooling)

what you need

150 g (5 oz) white
  chocolate

80 g (3¼ oz) unsalted
  butter

Double boiler, or
  heatproof bowl and
  saucepan (the bowl
  should sit snugly
  on top)

Wooden spoon

½ teaspoon vanilla
  essence

2 egg yolks, lightly
  beaten

Mixing bowl

Whisk

Pastry board

Clingfilm

Dessert spoon

40 g (1½ oz) icing sugar

Plate

Nonstick baking paper

Scissors

Coloured tissue paper

Gift box

white chocolate truffles

ages 6–8 years

Delicious vanilla-flavoured white chocolate truffles are a favourite with any chocolate lover. When you make them yourself, you don't have to save them up as a special treat; give them as a little present when a friend needs cheering up.

1 Roughly break up the chocolate. Cut the butter into small pieces. Slowly melt the chocolate and butter pieces in the double boiler or in the bowl on top of the saucepan filled with a little hot water. (An adult should be at hand to supervise.) Stir with the wooden spoon.

2 Remove from the heat and stir in the vanilla essence.

3 Tip the egg yolks into a mixing bowl. Gradually whisk the warm chocolate mixture into the eggs. Cover the bowl with clingfilm and place in the refrigerator for about 8 hours, to firm.

4 Place the chocolate mixture on a pastry board. Scoop up some of the mixture with the dessert spoon and roll between your palms into a ball. Repeat until you have used up the chocolate mixture.

5 Sprinkle the icing sugar over the plate. Roll the balls in the sugar and set on a sheet of baking paper.

6 Cut pieces of coloured tissue paper and baking paper just large enough to line the gift box. Cut the edges in a zig-zag shape. Place first the tissue paper, then the baking paper in the box. Fill the box with the truffles.

tips

★ Make sure you have cool hands when you roll the chocolate mixture into balls to prevent it from melting as you work. Run your hands under a cold tap and dry well if you find them warming up.

★ These truffles will keep for 5 days in a sealed container in the refrigerator. You could write this instruction on the bottom of the gift box with a pretty-coloured pen or on a label in your best handwriting.

variation

milk chocolate truffles

Instead of using white chocolate, substitute milk chocolate. Then, in step 5, roll the balls in grated chocolate rather than icing sugar.

Christmas tree cookies

ages 8–10 years

Tree-shaped biscuits look fabulously festive adorning a winter party table. You can decorate them with ready-made writing icing squeezed direct from a tube and lots of coloured sugar-coated chocolate beans (if you don't eat too many while you're sticking them on!).

1 Beat the butter and sugar together in the mixing bowl. Beat in the egg and stir in a few drops of vanilla essence.

2 Stir in the flour and baking powder, then knead the mixture into a firm dough on the pastry board. Wrap the dough in clingfilm and chill for one hour in the refrigerator.

3 Lightly flour a sheet of baking paper cut to fit the baking sheet. Roll the dough out flat on the pastry board, about 5 mm (¼ in) thick. Stamp out tree shapes with the cookie cutter. Transfer to the baking sheet.

4 Place the baking sheet in a preheated oven, 160°C (325°F), Gas Mark 3, for 15 minutes. (An adult should assist at this stage.) Remove from the oven and allow to cool on the wire rack.

5 Run a line of green icing in simple outlines on each tree biscuit. Press the sugar-coated chocolate beans onto the icing.

6 When the icing has set firm, place the cookies in a colourful box, ready to offer around to friends and family.

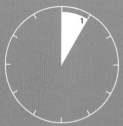

**time needed
1 hour**
(excluding chilling and baking)

what you need

Wooden spoon

125 g (4 oz) unsalted butter

125 g (4 oz) caster sugar

Mixing bowl

1 egg

Vanilla essence

275 g (9 oz) plain flour, plus extra for flouring

½ teaspoon baking powder

Pastry board

Clingfilm

Nonstick baking paper

Scissors

Baking sheet

Rolling pin

Tree-shaped cookie cutter

Wire rack

Green writing icing with fine nozzle

Sugar-coated chocolate beans

Colourful gift box

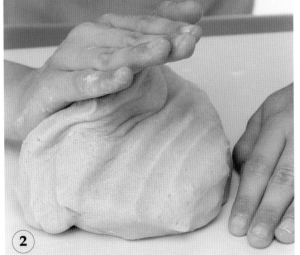

variation

festive bell biscuits

Stamp out bell shapes with a bell-shaped cookie cutter. Make a hole in the top of each one with a drinking straw so you can thread them with ribbon to hang on a tree.

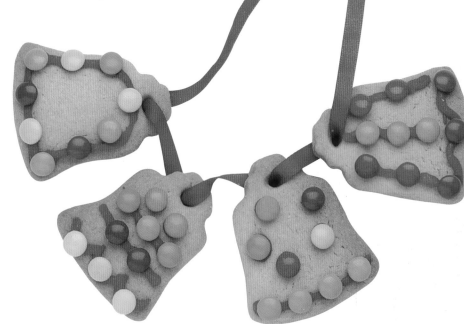

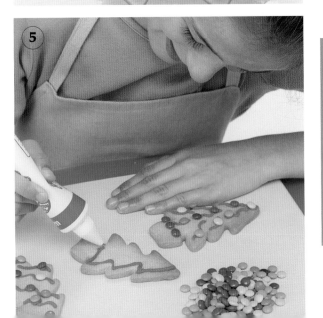

tip

★ Don't forget to stamp the hole for the ribbon before baking the biscuits: they will be too hard to pierce once baked.

★ These cookies will keep in a sealed container for one week.

flavoured oil

ages 6–8 years

Give extra flavour and visual interest to a bottle of olive oil by adding some peppercorns and fragrant herbs to the bottle. This gift is sure to inspire food lovers with its spicy flavourings.

**time needed
45 minutes**

what you need

Bottle of olive oil

Large bowl

Hot water

Handful of mixed peppercorns

1 bay leaf

Bunch of thyme

Scissors

Green card

Hole punch

Raffia

1 Remove the label from the bottle of olive oil by soaking it in hot water for 5 minutes before peeling off. Pour out a little of the olive oil from the bottle – about a quarter of a cup should do. Prise off the plastic pourer using a fork, if the bottle has one (an adult might need to help at this stage).

2 Drop a small handful of peppercorns into the bottle of olive oil.

3 Carefully push the bay leaf into the bottle. Then push in the bunch of thyme (remove any ties or elastic bands securing the stems first). Screw the bottle top on tightly and wipe away any spilt oil with a clean cloth.

4 Cut a bay leaf shape from the green card. Fold the leaf in half, then open it out flat again. Punch a hole at the top of the leaf.

5 Thread the leaf onto a few lengths of raffia. Tie the raffia around the top of the bottle.

2

3

variation

herby vinegar

Slip a bunch of tarragon into a bottle of white wine vinegar. Tie the leaf tag to the bottle with lengths of curling gift-wrapping ribbon, curling them by drawing a blunt knife out from the knot to the end of each length.

tip

★ Write a short message on the back of the leaf before fastening it to the bottle.

templates

On this and the following pages are all the templates required to make the projects in this book. All templates are shown actual size.

lavender sprigs

rose bud

bird clock

bird

flower

daffodil petal

flower

plant pot

daffodil leaf

star giftwrap variations

star

spotty dog ear

spotty dog head

spotty dog tail

foldline

spotty dog/pink pig/funny frog body

comb

eye

beak

hen egg cosy body

hen comb

hen beak

pig ear

pig head/muzzle

frog head

frog foot

insect wing

oak leaf

cat ear/bird beak

elephant ear

eye patch

tricorn hat

butterfly

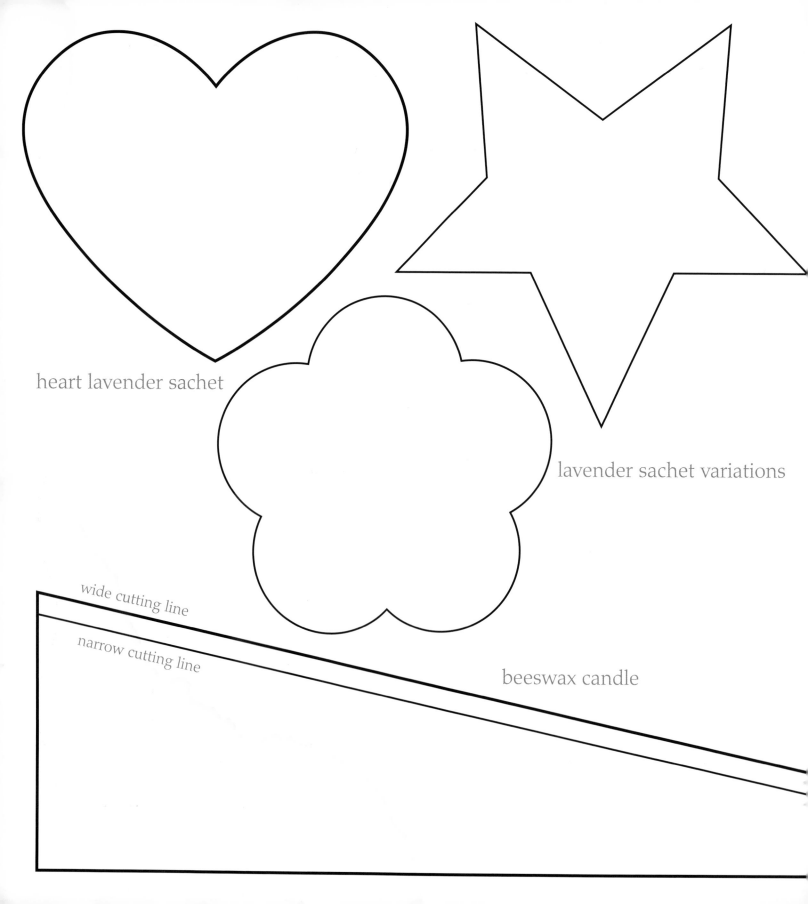

heart lavender sachet

lavender sachet variations

wide cutting line

narrow cutting line

beeswax candle

fish

shell

starfish

purse

bookmark

index

acknowledgements

The author and Publishers would like to thank Jemma Austin, Ellen Barnes, Jack Barnes, Yasmin Burgos-Cook, Ella-Joy Harrington, Katie Paul, Jack Prior, Martha-Mae Prior, Nina Roscoe, Sash Stuart, Gabriella Turk, Greg Williams, Zara Williams and Jemima Wood for being such fantastic models. A special thank you goes to Leslie and Mike Prior for all their help during the photo shoot.

Executive Editor Jane McIntosh

Editor Leanne Bryan

Executive Art Editor Joanna MacGregor

Designer One2six Creative

Production Manager Ian Paton

Photographer Mike Prior